add

D0475704

CULTURE
AND
COMMUNICATION

Publication Number 506

AMERICAN LECTURE SERIES®

Edited by

DOMINICK A. BARBARA, M.D., F.A.P.A.
Certified Practicing Psychoanalyst
Associated with the American Institute for Psychoanalysis
Fellow, American Psychiatric Association
Head of the Speech Department, Karen Horney Clinic
New York City

CULTURE AND COMMUNICATION

THE PROBLEM OF PENETRATING
NATIONAL AND CULTURAL BOUNDARIES

By

ROBERT T. OLIVER, Ph.D., LL.D.

Head, Department of Speech
The Pennsylvania State University
University Park, Pennsylvania

CHARLES C THOMAS · PUBLISHER
Springfield · Illinois · U.S.A.

CHARLES C THOMAS • PUBLISHER
BANNERSTONE HOUSE
301-327 East Lawrence Avenue, Springfield, Illinois, U.S.A.

© 1962, by CHARLES C THOMAS • PUBLISHER
Library of Congress Catalog Card Number: 62-12051

With THOMAS BOOKS careful attention is given to all details of manu-
facturing and design. It is the Publisher's desire to present books that are
satisfactory as to their physical qualities and artistic possibilities and appropriate for their particular use. THOMAS BOOKS will be true to those laws
of quality and assure a good name and good will.

Printed in the United States of America

THE LANGUAGE OF THE MIND

If we seek to understand a people, we have to try to put ourselves, as far as we can, in that particular historical and cultural background. . . . It is not easy for a person of one country to enter into the background of another country. So there is great irritation, because one fact that seems obvious to us is not immediately accepted by the other party or doesn't seem obvious to him at all. . . . But that extreme irritation will go when we think . . . that he is just differently conditioned and simply can't get out of that condition. . . . One has to recognize that whatever the future may hold, countries and peoples differ in their approach and their ways, in their approach to life and their ways of living and thinking. In order to understand them we have to understand their way of life and approach. If we wish to convince them, we have to use their language as far as we can, not language in the narrow sense of the word, but the language of the mind. That is one necessity. Something that goes even much further than that is not the appeal to logic and reason, but some kind of emotional awareness of the other people.—

JAWAHARLAL NEHRU: *Visit to America*
New York, John Day Co., 1950, pp. 58-59.

BOOKS

by

Robert T. Oliver

Culture and Communication: The Problem of Penetrating National and Cultural
Boundaries

The Healthy Mind in Communion and Communication (With Dr. Dominick A.
Barbara, M.D.)

Conversation: The Development and Expression of Personality

Four Who Spoke Out: Burke, Fox, Sheridan, and Pitt

Psychology of Persuasive Speech

Syngman Rhee: The Man Behind the Myth

Training for Effective Speech

Effective Speech (with R. L. Cortright)

Communicative Speech (with H. P. Zelko and P. D. Holtzman)

Developing Ideas for Essays and Speeches (with H. W. Robbins)

Effective Speech Notebook

Persuasive Speaking: Principles and Methods

Korea: Forgotten Nation

Why War Came in Korea

The Truth about Korea

Verdict in Korea

Effective Speech for Democratic Living

Korea My Country, by Young Tai Pyun (Editor)

Re-Establishing the Speech Profession: The First Fifty Years (Editor, with M. G.
Bauer)

PREFACE

Recent anthropological research indicates that the human race originated some 1,500,000 years ago. Today, for the first time in all that vast procession of 45,000 generations, we face the positive danger that the entire race of man may be extinguished. The means of total destruction exist—and are in the control of a very small number of individuals. There is always the chance that some one of them could willfully or accidentally unloose forces never to be stopped until the entire globe should have become a gruesome waste of radio-active ruins unfit for human habitation.

Nor is this the final measure of our danger. The production and control of these means of destruction cannot possibly be confined to their present masters. France has recently joined the Atomic Club. Red China is nearing the threshold. Everything we know about the permeability of scientific knowledge warns us that the ability to manufacture atomic and hydrogen weapons (and their successors) will very shortly, measured in historical time, be spread so widely that scarcely a dictator anywhere will lack access to this means of blackmail and this potentiality of complete disaster.

Time, which always has been man's most precious commodity, is truly running out. The technology of war has cast a lurid glow of menace across the pages of the very calendar we hold in hand—now, today.

Meanwhile, the differences of race and culture that traditionally have divided mankind into mutually suspicious groups have become not less but more susceptible of explosion during this past generation in which modern communication has brought together but has failed to unite the peoples of the world. Across the face of the globe, from the beginnings of time, have been drawn artificial barriers that divide tribes or nations into sharply separated segments: separated by race, by religion, by contrasting cultural patterns, and by wide disparity of individual and social welfare. The first duty of every State is assumed to be the maintenance of the ability to make war—to defend itself and, if need be, to fight for what it believes to be its rights.

In our own time, this age-old comfortable compartmentalization of nations, of races, and of cultures has visibly become obsolescent and, predictably, is nearing an end. The time has come when we must become "all one thing or all another." We can live together or we can be dead together. There no longer is a viable choice of continuing to live apart.

Peoples whose ancestors have been impoverished and illiterate for multiple centuries have, in the aftermath of World War II, been swept pell-mell into the swirling current of at least partial enlightenment concerning current affairs. They now know about New York, and Paris, and London. They know about bathtubs, and automobiles, and television. They know about over-full granaries, and refrigerators, and weight reduction diets. They know about health, and wealth, and the problem of what to do with leisure time. And they know, too, of the recessive and barbaric hatreds and fears and revulsions against darker skins, and crinkly hair, and slanted eyes.

The veil of secrecy has been withdrawn. Within the close eye-view of the hungry two billions is the over-rich surplus of abundance of the top-half of the other billion. On both sides of the divide it is now understood that two-thirds of humanity is under-nourished, under-educated, and under-privileged. They and we alike realize that while our most urgent personal problem is how to reduce, their most urgent personal problem is how to survive. Before the eyes of the black, and brown, and yellow races is spread the daily record of the proud assertion of innate superiority by the small minority of whites. And as they are learning about us, so are we learning about them. Effective coordination of common goals and methods is still to be developed; but all mankind is confronting the urgent need to put an end to the imbalance and maldistribution of attainable well-being.

Knowing more and more about one another has not lessened, but has increased, the tensions and the problems. Racial, religious, and national antipathies have become fully as explosive and danger-ous as are the atomic and hydrogen bombs. In this respect, too, the calendar has become fearfully fore-shortened. The time within which we must solve our problems of prejudice and achieve a genuinely all-inclusive mutuality of understanding and appreciation among the diverse peoples of the world is already all but wholly consumed. Tomorrow becomes a word upon which we cannot much longer comfortably depend.

Still another problem is hastening to add yet further complexities to our problem of learning how to live together. This is the weird phenomenon we call the "population explosion." It is a sobering thought that one of every ten human beings who have ever lived on earth are alive today. Medical science has expanded wonderfully the life-span of human beings, while procreation is multiplying new births at a rate never before imagined. China's four hundred millions of 1920 have become seven hundred millions and continue to mount at the rate of forty-five to fifty millions each year. Overcrowding is a growing threat in all Asia today and in all the world tomorrow. *Lebensraum* has ceased to be merely a pretext for imperialism and has become the desperate cry of all humanity. Within a generation two billions of human beings have become three; and within another two generations there will be five billions of us. Where it may end (unless it be in suicidal battle for the bare means of survival) no one can safely estimate.

Remedial measures, of course, are not lacking. Vast new food supplies wait to be harvested from the seas. Salt water will shortly yield its salinity to the new technology, so that it may be used to water the deserts and multiply the productivity of the land. Atomic power will replace the rapidly diminishing resources of coal and oil. Plastics will substitute in some measure for vanishing wood and iron. Human ingenuity is working desperate miracles in a frantic race to keep up with the needs.

Meanwhile, every new advance in humane science prolongs old lives and preserves new ones. Under-developed nations achieve amazing advances, yet lag further and further behind the rising spiral of added population. Our splendid age of tremendous production is becoming paradoxically also an age of spreading slums and of creeping hunger. Even in the promising periphery of modernism in the Latin American nations, at their present rate of ec-

onomic growth it will take them two hundred and fifty years even
to attain a level of welfare one-third as great as is now·enjoyed in
the United States. In many other areas, even this kind of prospect
seems chimerical. In the race between increasing population and
the inventing of synthetic substitutes for natural resources, time is
slipping by so rapidly that our very children will confront scenes
of despoiliation still mercifully concealed from our imagination.

Because of problems of this nature, which are common to mankind, it is all the more tragic that the separated divisions of humanity remain unable to speak to one another with mutual comprehension. We cannot solve our problems unless or until we can
discuss them. We cannot expect mankind to unite in a common
struggle for survival until there develops a premise and a methodology of communion. Community depends upon communication.
This is the problem to which this book is addressed.

Many idealists and many scholars have concerned themselves
with the need for a world-wide language. English has long been a
leading candidate for this function—because it is spoken natively
by more people than is any other tongue; because of its importance
politically and economically; and because of its recreational appeal
through the Hollywood movies and on television film. Recently the
Russian language has improved its global position through the
spread of Communism and the rapid growth of Russian science
and technology. Meanwhile, sporadic but earnest efforts have been
made to popularize such artificial "second languages" as Esperan-
to, Ido, Volapuk, Interlingua, Novillo, Lingo, and others. But,
laudable though such efforts may be, they are countered by the
nationalistic spirit that has virtually doubled the number of na-
tion-states within the past decade, each with a fiercely assertive
pride in its own traditions, its own culture, and, similarly, in its
own language.

With modern means of simultaneous translation, linguistic
barriers as such are actually coming to appear less formidable than
in earlier times. Of course, there always will remain a rich residue
of meaning that defies transliteration from one language to another.
There is staunch truth in the dictum of Robert Frost that "Poetry
is what remains untouched by translation." The emotional bonds

that exist within language communities are always different from and stronger than the bridges that may be constructed across chasms of linguistic differences. No one doubts that it would be a vast convenience if the whole human race could be brought to speak a common tongue. But we also recognize that the likelihood of this ideal ever being achieved is less than promising. Even if its achievement is ultimately conceivable, it surely will not be accomplished in time to help much with the problems that press urgently upon us.

But even if by some miracle the gift of common speech could somehow suddenly be achieved, the basic problem of incommunicability would not thereby be solved. For mankind is separated less by language barriers (grievous though they are) than it is by cultural differences. Not only do we not speak alike, but, more importantly, we do not think alike. Every separate community has its own value system. Every culture has its own modes of thought and its own selected interest areas which constitute the subject matter it chooses to think about. The ways in which the mind of a Hindu differ in its workings from the mind of an American are more complex and more basic than the differences between the Hindi and the English languages. Moulds of traditional thought patterns are rooted far more deeply than in vocabulary and grammar. We are vastly in need of broader linguistic skills; but our need is even stronger for common understandings and insights. And while we can not or will not share a communal system of values, there is all the more urgent need to realize what the differences are and why they exist.

The aim of this book is to indicate something of the diversity of goals and methods which mark the nature of separate nations and separate cultures, and to suggest some directions we should follow in seeking to bridge them. To try to present the problem in full clarity or to attempt to outline a method for global communicativeness would be the height of folly. We stand merely at the threshold of the new frontier of One-Worldliness. Many initial explorations must precede dependable mapping of the territory of mutuality which we are just now commencing to think about. There can be no entry into the new era until we are acutely aware of the pitfalls and come to understand both the differences and the similarities of the major culture systems. The task is inevitably one that calls for many minds working at the problem over a period of many years.

Neither is it claimed that this book constitutes a pioneer venture into this frontier. The whole science of anthropology is devoted to it. Such philosophic interpretations as Will Durant's *Our Oriental Heritage* and F. S. C. Northrop's *The Meeting of East and West* have made notable advances in the direction of global understanding. Multiple volumes have dealt with the impact of one culture upon another or of the troublesome efforts of individuals to move from one culture into another. Meanwhile, a rapidly expanding library of books and articles on propaganda and psychological warfare is being written. The problem that gave rise to this book is not new; it is for many people the central problem of our age.

Nevertheless, the justification for this volume is that nowhere will the reader encounter any other that is like it. In a unique sense it has grown (as all books must) from the experience and the observations of its author. During a span of some twenty years I have travelled twelve times to the Orient, once to Australia, and three times to Europe and the Middle East, with peripheral trips to Canada and Mexico. During much of that time I have served as a consultant at international conferences and have worked with the Republic of Korea, on questions affecting its relations with the United States and the United Nations. My own inquiry during this time has been directed to two questions: how does one government speak effectively to others; and how do people from one culture communicate their needs and aspirations to peoples of other cultures? The problems have always been practical ones, and pragmatic answers have been required.

Gradually, two convictions have grown strong. The first of these is that the kind of thought that matters most is *rhetorical*—which is to say, the way in which a people views any problem in terms of its own purposes and its own estimate of the nature of its chosen audience. What is ultimately true about a given subject is, in international relations, often of less instant import than what must be done and said in order to be persuasive in relation to it. The rhetorical approach, then, concerns the manner in which one set of spokesmen from one community try to influence the reactions of another set from a different cultural entity. What is important *to us* concerning Communism, or Confucianism, and Taoism, and Hinduism is, first of all, their rhetorical characteristics. By what modes do they strive to persuade; and by what means may they be persuaded? In part this involves the rules of the game called diplomacy—the game which is predicated on the sovereignty of nations—and this is one theme of the chapters that follow.

The second conviction that has led to the writing of this book is that there is sound truth in the famous French maxim: *Plus ça change, plus c'est la même chose.* Beneath the swirling surface changes which occur with bewildering speed there lie fundamental cultural characteristics that change ever so slowly—in terms of multiple centuries, rather than day-by-day. From this point of view it is concluded that to rightly understand the neutralism of Nehru we need to know not merely the need of India for more iron and steel production today but also the tenacity with which Indians cling to a value system that is already forty and fifty centuries old.

The point is often over-looked, but it is not new. Keurs, for example, has illuminated it with his study of *The Deeply Rooted,* an analysis of a Netherlands community. Alwyn Rees, in *Life in a Welsh Countryside,* shows how centuries-old customs persist despite industrialization. The whole point of studying history resides in the belief that modern-day Western man has to be contemplated in terms of the "social conglomerate" accumulated from the civilizations of Athens, Israel, Rome, and the Middle Ages.

The point has recently been reiterated by Dr. Alexander Lessing, Chairman of the Department of Sociology in Hofstra College, writing in the October, 1961, issue of the quarterly *Midway,* where he says: "Such obstinate endurance, with its inner resistance to engulfment by dominant but alien traditions, can be understood, no doubt, as a reflection of the fundamental role of primary relationships—especially that of parents and children—in handing on basic attitudes, feelings, and patterns of interpersonal relations.

But it is also a stubborn fact of vital importance in understanding
the contemporary world of many peoples and many cultures, each
of whom may seek from the West ways to improve the standards of
life, but each of whom may at the same time be determined to keep
an identity and tradition of its own."

Here is the point: if we are to deal effectively with the other
peoples of the world, we must do it realistically in terms of the
methodologies that work in the diplomatic exchanges between and
among sovereign nations—which are significantly different from
the way individual deals with individual. This is one topic of the
following pages. Moreover, when we talk with them about the
problems that make headlines in today's newspapers, we must
penetrate through and behind these questions, down into the
substratum of their principles and feelings, which are rooted in
ancient ways of thinking and feeling. This is the second topic of
the chapters that follow. The two problems are interrelated.
Separately, they are the concern of political scientists on the one
hand and of anthropologists on the other. Viewed together, they
are in the province of rhetoric.

Whatever this study has, then, that is really new lies in its
rhetorical mode of inquiry. From this point of view, many questions are raised, some of them new. A few tentative answers are
suggested as worthy of further exploration. The time has not yet
arrived when it is possible to present a handbook of international
community. But the time has urgently come when the means of talking meaningfully together as a global community must be searched
out. For some readers this book may serve as an introduction to a
new way of thinking about international relations. To others it
may do no more than help fill in a few chinks. Its subject matter
can fail to be of interest only to those who are willfully blind to
the nature of the time in which we live.

ACKNOWLEDGMENTS

INEVITABLY, MANY PEOPLE contribute to the writing of any book, particularly one such as this. I am grateful to the many scholars, translators, and philosophical writers whose works have helped me formulate the concepts presented in these pages. Special appreciation is extended to the Republic of Korea, and particularly to Dr. and Mrs. Syngman Rhee, Mr. Pyun Yung Tai, Colonel Ben C. Limb, and Pyo-Wook and Chungnim Han, for the opportunities they have afforded me to participate in and to discuss with them the problems of international relations. Thanks are also gratefully extended to the Pennsylvania State University for its grant of released time and its support through the Fund for Research Studies, which have facilitated completion of this work. To my wife and sons I am grateful for the sly questions and doubtful pauses with which they often encouraged me to "look again" at various concepts and interpretations.

I am grateful to K. N. S. Rao for his reading of the three chapters on Orientalism and to Dr. Pandhari-Nath Prabhu, of Gujarat University, Ahmedabad, for helpful comments on the chapter on India.

I want to thank especially Ambassador Limb, Consul-General Smith, and Dr. Vinocour, as well as the editors of the *Quarterly Journal of Speech*, *Today's Speech*, and *Western Speech*, for the graciousness with which they consented to the use in this book of their articles. Portions of the book, other than these three chapters, have also been rewritten from articles of my own which appeared in the *Quarterly Journal of Speech*, the *Southern Speech Journal*, the *Central States Speech Journal*, *Western Speech*, and *Vital Speeches of the Day*.

R. T. O.

CONTENTS

CULTURE
AND
COMMUNICATION

Chapter 1

THE ROLE OF SPEECH IN DIPLOMACY

T HE SUBJECT OF THIS book is in part the relation between words and war. To put the same matter in other words, our concern is with ideas directed across national boundary lines. Some of the speech of international diplomacy is intended to prevent wars; in a sense the traditional view is that the job of the diplomat ends where the job of the general begins. Some diplomatic speech is intended to lay a basis for starting a war—to mobilize public opinion for an approaching conflict. Another purpose of international speech, especially in this era of mass communication, is to win wars without battle. Subversion and propaganda are devised to weaken the will to resist aggression, to create dissension and disloyalty within an enemy nation, to show the futility of further resistance, and to persuade potential allies to remain neutral or to help the aggressor.

Winston Churchill emphasized the role of diplomatic speech in avoiding or at least postponing wars by his famous comment that "jaw jaw is better than war war." Dwight Eisenhower, at the Summit Conference in Geneva, in 1956, stated flatly that "There is no alternative to peace"—indicating that in our Atomic Age diplomacy must somehow find solutions that in former times were finally hammered out on battlefields. As long ago as July 26, 1906, William Jennings Bryan, speaking at the Inter-Parliamentary Union in London, declared hopefully: "I am glad the time is coming when public opinion is to be more and more powerful . . . when the world will insist that nations settle their differences by some peaceful means." Many have echoed his contention that modern means of transporting weapons have made peace essential and that modern means of communication have made it possible. The reasoning is that since on a global scale we can now talk together, we can understand one another; and that understanding is the matrix for conciliation and friendship. Will Rogers touched a wellspring of sympathetic response when he said, "I never met a man I didn't like." And many people have shared a conviction

3

that if only nations can talk over their problems they need not fight over them. But we are also confronted by the somber reminder of Secretary of State Dean Rusk that, "The United Nations has fallen somewhat short of our expectations for it."

Since the hopeful plea of William Jennings Bryan, the world has suffered more from the desolation of war than in any previous era of history. Talk so far has not prevented fighting, although in some specific situations it may have averted specific conflicts. On the other hand, there is ample reason to doubt the validity of Churchill's judgment that "jaw jaw is better than war war." The totalitarian dictatorships—notably Nazism and Communism—have demonstrated that speech used as a weapon of aggression is perhaps fully as effective an instrument of imperialistic conquest as are marching armies. Freedom can be lost without the firing of a shot —or the shots may be merely mopping up operations after the essential conquest has already been achieved by psychological means.

In the speech by which Woodrow Wilson presented his "Fourteen Points" for making the world safe for peaceful democracy, he uneasily confessed: "If the direct relation of peoples to peoples which modern communications permit are relations of understanding . . . then peace will work. If, however, the direct relations of people with each other are relations of doubt . . ." It was not long before the world was to find that the more nations learn of the purposes of one another, the more they become doubtful and suspicious. The lesson was first driven home by the Communist revolution in Russia, as Isaac Deutscher pointed out in his 1954 book, *The Prophet Armed,* in which he said: ". . . in this revolution words, great idealistic words, were in fact more effective than regiments and divisions, and inspired tirades did the work of pitched battles. . . . The revolution worked mainly through its titantic powers of persuasion."

How this new warfare of words was to work was spelled out by Nickolai Lenin, when he told his followers that "Communist parties must strive unceasingly for power; and to achieve it they must know how to combine the strictest loyalty to the ideas of Communism with an ability to make all the practical compromises

—to attack, make agreements, zigzags, retreats, and so on. Revolutionaries who are not prepared for such accommodations are very bad revolutionaries." Joseph Stalin added his approval: "Tactics change according to flow and ebb." And Nikita Khrushchev added to this advice on how to confound the enemies of Communism a defense of the censorship imposed at home, as a barrier against appeals directed by the democracies to the Russian people. In a speech at Krasnoyarsk, Siberia, on October 11, 1959, he said: "They want to foist upon us all kinds of trash that would poison the minds of the Soviet people. Can we agree to this? Of course not! Our people do not want to consume bad food poisoned with the venom of bourgeois ideas." An editorial in *Pravda*, on July 6, 1956, made explicit the complete control of internal information as a means of maintaining the will to struggle and sacrifice for world domination: "As concerns our country, the Communist party was, is, and will be the only sovereign of the thoughts, spokesman of the ideas and aspirations, director and organizer of the people during the entire duration of its struggle for communism."

In *Mein Kampf*, which Adolf Hitler published in 1925 as a guide for his Nazi followers, the essential immorality of the war of words was set forth most blatantly, as he analyzed the kind of verbal weapon that is most effective: ". . . in the size of the lie there is a certain factor of credibility, since the broad mass of the people will be more easily corrupted in the depths of their hearts than they will be consciously and intentionally evil. Consequently, with the primitive simplicity of their feelings they fall victim more easily to a big lie than to a small one, since they themselves occasionally lie in small matters but they would be ashamed to tell great lies. Such a falsehood will not enter their minds, and they will also not be able to imagine others asserting the great boldness of the most infamous misrepresentations. And even with the explanation of the matter, they long hesitate and vacillate and accept at least some ground as true; consequently, from the most bold lie, something will remain . . ."

The well-known public relations counsellor, Edward Bernays, has with reason warned us that the United States lags at least twenty-five years behind the Communists in our understanding of the nature of propaganda. Yet this is an area of international relations that may prove to be at least as important as the missile race—perhaps more so, if it should turn out that the world struggle is to be finally determined without recourse to another major war.

The nature of our dilemma was stated with remarkable clarity by Demosthenes, speaking to the Assembly of Athens, some twenty-five hundred years ago. "Ambassadors," Demosthenes said, "have no battleships at their disposal, or heavy infantry, or fortresses; their weapons are words and opportunities. In important transactions, opportunities are fleeting; once they are missed they cannot be recovered." He went on to point out that autocracies are better suited than are democracies to seize upon advantages that arise in critical situations. "Under their systems, action can be taken instantly and on the word of command; but with us, first the Council has to be notified and adopt a provisional resolution, and even then only when the heralds and Ambassadors have sent in a note in writing. Then the Council has to convene the Assembly, but then only on a statutory date. Then the debater has to prove his case in the face of an ignorant and often corrupt opposition; and even when this endless procedure has been completed, and a decision has been come to, even more time is wasted before the necessary financial resolution can be passed. Thus an Ambassador, who, in a constitution such as ours, acts in a dilatory manner and causes us to miss our opportunities, is not missing opportunities only, but robbing us of the control of events."

Demosthenes did not wish to make the point that democracy is inferior to dictatorship—even in time of crisis. What he did intend was to help his listeners understand the peculiar nature of the difficulties of diplomatic speech. He wished also to arouse them to an awareness of the great danger that their nation might be lost even without an armed attack against it. His concern was the greater since he doubted whether his listeners were "conscious even of the elaborate methods by which your country is slowly being undermined."

In this present work, attention is directed only incidentally to the means by which our nation and our way of life are "slowly being undermined." Instead, the problem considered is the means by which our own vibrant belief in democracy can be effectively transmitted to other peoples. How can we talk, with effect, across international boundary lines? How can we properly estimate the complex task which is faced by our Voice of America and our diplomats? How can we better understand their difficulties and thus better interpret the degree of their success or failure? How can we, ordinary citizens, in our own contacts with foreign nations (or, indeed, in our own behavior here at home) do more to help and less to hinder the cause of international acceptance of our American ideal?

Frequently the directors of our own propaganda mechanisms declare that their only method is to tell the truth and let the chips fall where they may. They insist that, in our policy, propaganda is a very simple matter—a mere matter of honest reporting of all the relevant facts, with the hope that somehow there will result an understanding that is both correct and sympathetic. In this assertion of their own method they do themselves less than justice. The job of representing our nation abroad is exceedingly complex; if no more than transparent honesty were needed, any number of farmers' boys could be sent to do the job.

A more accurate statement of the dilemma confronted by our public spokesmen was made by the English economist, John Maynard Keynes, in his *Essays in Persuasion,* where he wryly noted the "obligation" of Cabinet Ministers to "sacrifice veracity to the public weal." He declared that "It is the method of modern statesmen to talk as much folly as the public demand and to practice no more of it than is compatible with what they have said, trusting that such folly in action as must wait upon folly in word will soon disclose itself as such, and furnish an opportunity for slipping back into wisdom." In Keynes' view, the folly of utterance is demanded by the fact that "public passions and public ignorance play a part in the world of which he who aspires to lead a democracy must take account." Even if we feel that plain thinking and plain talking are the best devices for winning international friends and influencing policies, we yet may be forced to agree that just as bad money drives good money out of circulation, so does the duplicity of the propaganda of totalitarianism tend to make impossible the frank and candid give-and-take of honest negotiation.

Still another problem of diplomatic speech in our time was high-lighted by Lester Pearson, when he was Foreign Minister of Canada, in his observation that "Open diplomacy now tends to be frozen diplomacy." When international discussion has to take place in the open meetings of the United Nations, or in the essentially open meetings of special conferences—where the pretense is elaborately maintained of keeping proceedings secret—diplomats are restrained by the public opinion of their home audiences from retreating from positions once stated. Debate replaces discussion and propaganda replaces diplomacy. This is as true for us as it is for our opponents, though we commonly direct the charge against them—perhaps because they are more skilled in their propaganda than we have been in ours.

There is little point in concerning ourselves with the relative weight of diplomatic persuasion on the one hand and military power on the other as counters in the global struggle. Whether the tongue is mightier than the atomic bomb is no better than an academic question. The influence of both are being used as well as the skills of diplomats on both sides of the Iron Curtain permit. Those who coin and use phrases are as truly warriors in the arena of international conflict as are those who manufacture or plan the strategic use of guided missiles.

The speech of diplomacy and of propaganda is subject to strategic considerations as rigorous and complex as those applied to armed forces. Amateurs with words can cause, and on occasion have caused, as much damage and tragic waste as have amateurs in military commands. Knowing what to say and how and when to say it is often of an importance parallel to knowing what kinds of armed force to mobilize and when and how to employ them. Psychological warfare has emerged from theory to practice. Total war destroys minds and souls as well as bodies, warps hopes as well as wounding limbs. And "cold" war has proved more effective at less cost than "hot" wars often have.

More broadly, our concern should be not alone with psychological warfare but with a wide range of psychological operations. Our international speech is directed not only to defeating enemies but also to winning friends. We not only wage "cold" wars but we also wage "warm" persuasive campaigns. Our diplomatic speech has no less a role to play in building confidence in our cause in Africa, and the Middle East, and South America than it has in deterring Communist attacks against the fledgling nations of Southeast Asia. How to talk winningly is as important to understand as how to talk warningly.

Both the formation and the application of psychological policies in this gigantic international field of competition and conflict are the responsibilities of a broad category of officials—much broader than the direct representatives accredited to foreign nations who have traditionally been thought of as our diplomats. The speech functions which they must serve are manifold. They involve the careful and considered use of public address, private consultations, and group conferences. They must seek to influence their own "home" audience, varying enemy audiences, and an extremely diverse group of neutral audiences. They must take into account fundamental divisions within each of these three loose categories. They must phrase ideas adequately to meet contingencies that are all but impossible to foretell. They must speak with enough authority to carry conviction, yet with caution enough to guard meanwhile against the probability of policy reversals. Whatever they say must be well tailored to the essential context in which their remarks are delivered; but they realize that, meanwhile, in other contexts their words will do far more harm than good.

Official spokesmen for government policies must avoid "war mongering" or "reckless talk of the possibilities of war," on the one hand; and on the other they must just as carefully avoid "peace mongering," or "reckless talk of the possibilities of peace." They dare not arouse a war-like spirit that they may later be unable to dissipate, control, support, or direct; and they must equally avoid arousing a determination for peace which might cause unpreparedness or unwillingness to meet potential dangers.

One of their indispensable functions is the creation of stereotyped reactions to world circumstances and events. This is to say that they must seek to develop a total and overwhelming singleness of response to such circumstances as the Communist occupation of China and to such events as a threatened or actual attack against another free nation. Yet there are grave dangers in carrying out this function. In the first place, the stereotyped responses they need from their home audience, from the enemy audience, and from the audience of neutrals may all differ widely. Secondly, because of this disparity, the accomplishment of their purpose in dramatizing a particular stereotyped understanding at home may have very undesirable results abroad. Thirdly, since international affairs are subject to rapid changes, there may occur almost overnight a fundamental change in the kind of stereotyped reactions required to serve our policies.

United States domestic politics began a generation ago to feel the effects of revolutionary changes brought about by telegraphic news services, then the radio, and finally by television. No longer is it possible for a presidential candidate to address a localized group of voters without serious regard for the effect of what he says upon the entire nation. The problems of campaigning, consequently, became much more difficult. Attempts are always made, of course, to suggest appeals especially designed for particular sections; but on the whole the national campaigns have had to do what they can to submerge, to side-step, or to rise above regional differences. This has been done chiefly by two means. The first is to seek to concentrate the attention of the voters upon platitudes acceptable to all groups. The second has been to try to discover some vital issues upon which a decisive majority may be brought into agreement. Issues of this nature commonly lie in the realm of international affairs—and majority agreement is most easily achieved by attitudes of belligerence. Consequently, the very means used by domestic politicians (abroad as well as in the United States) compound the problems faced by our diplomats. With national elections taking place every two years, there is a constant stream of damage needing to be repaired.

Since the nineteen-thirties, when substantially the whole world was joined in one mass-communications radio network, diplomats have been subjected to this same revolution. In comparison to candidates for national office, they are severely handicapped in their attempts to re-adjust their thinking and their methods to this world situation. In the first place, there are comparatively few platitudes that have both world-wide acceptance and sufficient vitality to be realistically effective. The division of the world between the communistic and democratic ideologies is the most harrowing example. And, in the second place, the positions from which diplomats can formulate and state their policies are subject to the strains and stresses of domestic politics. Whatever politicians must do to attain or maintain power at home, diplomats must adjust to in their communications with foreign governments and other peoples. If a southern governor can only win election through a blatant "white supremacy" campaign, and if southern congressmen hold a balance of voting power on State Department appropriations and appointments, what a diplomat can say in Africa about race conflicts in Alabama is narrowly restricted. Similar influences are always exerted upon the diplomatic positions taken by spokesmen for other nations, however little we may understand this fact.

It is evident that the speech of diplomacy is subject to almost intolerable difficulties. It is no wonder that long and agonized preparation is required for the preparation of specific foreign policy statements and for the holding of international conferences. The halting uncertainties in parts of our foreign policy formulations are wholly explicable in terms of the problems of fitting what must be said to its varied audiences. But this does not mean that the difficulties should be accepted as excuses for failures that have occurred. It should, rather, call for increased efforts to solve the problems. It ought to mean that the highest skills of experts in speech and of foreign affairs experts should be joined. Perhaps it is impractical to produce experts in speech who are also experts in international relations; if so, the converse is probably also true. Certainly recent world events appear to indicate that our success in the use of diplomatic speech has been less than the situation demands. One remedy might be to combine the two types of expertness through group conferences on top administrative levels, where foreign policies are formulated and phrased.

The sheer bulk of the speaking diplomats must do (as is indicated in the chapters by Ambassador Limb and Consul-General Simpson) is sufficient to indicate the importance of this part of their diplomatic functions. The variety of types of speech skills which they require is another indication of the need for special training. Often the most important and usually the most difficult speech of diplomacy consists of public addresses—which, in veiw of modern publicity methods, have at least potentially a worldwide audience. The most futile of all diplomatic speech, under the conditions of enmity that underlie the major world divisions, would seem to be that devoted to international conferences. Meanwhile, by far the greatest amount of diplomatic speaking occurs in person-to-person consultations. At all levels, from top to bottom of national hierarchies, there are many daily meetings between representatives of one government and another. In many instances, these may involve a number of participants, but they remain on a person-to-person basis since there are always "two sides," with a leading spokesman for each. The techniques governing this kind of speaking have been worked out through many generations, and involve almost countless aspects.

In such speaking it is considered of prime importance to achieve the correct "level" of consultation. The representative of one government, for instance, must ordinarily insist upon consulting with an official of the other government whose rank and authority are at least as high as his own. This is not a mere quibbling over protocol, but involves the deepest considerations of the sovereign relationship of States. If the concept of "equality" is not maintained, the whole theory of sovereign power crumbles.

Secondly, the precise degree of hostility, friendship, or indifference that is to be expressed must be reckoned in advance, and overtly expressed. The language of diplomacy has been widely misunderstood as consisting principally of sweet words and blandishments. Quite to the contrary, it often consists of extreme brusqueness or of patent indifference. The latter may take the form of keeping an appointee waiting for ten or fifteen minutes, while the official he is to see may be observed through an open door shuffling papers at his desk. It is readily transmitted, as teachers of speech well know, by bodily posture and tones of voice.

As we confront the world beyond our own boundaries and try to talk with it, we cannot fail to be impressed by the fact that Russia appears to accomplish more by "talking tough" than we do by trying to be soothingly conciliatory. Often, it would appear, more is to be gained by threats than by friendship. This condition is not unique to the relationships of nations. All of us know that, as individuals, we can maintain friendly relations only on a basis of mutual consideration. If someone is trying to rape our wife, or kidnap our children, or cheat us in business, or force us out of the community, we can not counteract such behavior by soft words. We need to meet threat with threat, force with force. What is required for effective relations between nations, as between individuals, is not, *prima facie,* that we insist upon being friendly. What is required is that we truly understand them, and that we try to insure that they understand us. Our talk needs to reflect the reality of their intentions and of ours—and of the facts as they exist. This is one of the chief lessons that is often ignored as we wage our spluttering war of propaganda. Let us talk across national and cultural boundaries in terms that are true to the facts and true to the nature of the peoples whom we address. We already have an abundance of good will. What we most need now is a greater clarity of understanding.

In any event, the communication between the two governmental representatives is not at all upon a personal basis. Each is speaking for his own government, according to policies in the formulation of which he may have had a very minor part, if any at all. Neither is seeking to ingratiate himself with the other. Each is earnestly attempted to convey the precise shadings of feeling and understanding required by the policies he has come to represent. The conference fails or succeeds primarily to the extent to which those precise shadings are understood and transmitted to the higher levels of the hierarchy.

Under such circumstances, the ordinary rules and techniques

of "good" speech may actually prove more of a handicap than a help. The thinking of the diplomat must be based squarely upon the understanding that "speech is effective solely in terms of its total context." Effective technique for one conference may prove atrociously bad if used in another that may follow it thirty minutes later. The art of sensitively reacting to every shade of meaning, by whatever means it is conveyed, is essential. The diplomat must be skilled not only in speaking, but in listening and interpreting.

The diplomat must know, too, beyond any cavil, the prime necessity for the utmost precision in formulating his objectives for every speech or conference. Seldom—probably never—is any major goal achieved in one meeting. Many speeches and many speakers, on many very different occasions, are required before the desired end result is achieved. Careful analysis is required of what has occurred in any one speech session, in order to determine on what basis the succeeding effort should be made. In terms such as these, the old familiar advice we have so long repeated to our students to "limit the speech purpose and phrase it precisely" takes on deeper cogency and added significance.

Obviously, too, in conference situations the only kind of speech that can be used is the extemporaneous type. Preparation must be total—involving audience analysis, self-preparation, and thorough mastery of the subject in all its aspects and implications. Each speaker must seek to know more about all phases of the subject than does his conferee. While a modicum of bluff is certainly used, a diplomatic conference is similar, in many respects, to the trial of the Hindu Fakir in walking through a bed of red-hot stones: it is well to know precisely where it is safe to step!

In final summary of what is necessarily a hasty survey of a most important field, it may be said that speech lies at the very core of diplomacy. Basic policies are always decided in conferences among many advisors. Strategy in achieving the desired ends is again subject to group discussion and often to group decision. The steps necessary to achieve the objectives are a combination of force and persuasion. In the long run, the highest success is won by the diplomatic team best able to implant the most effective stereotyped judgments in the minds of the three audiences always ultimately addressed in diplomatic speaking. Diplomacy utilizes many means, but fundamental among them is *speech*. The speech of diplomacy is a vital factor in the relationship of our nation with both our enemies and our friends. As the currents of international relations in our time clearly indicate, there is urgent necessity that this problem should not be ignored.

Chapter 2

WHO ARE THE DIPLOMATS?

In Chapter 1 we have referred not only to diplomacy but also to propaganda. The Voice of America was mentioned and it was indicated that our concern is with the impact of ideas upon peoples of other nations, as well as upon governments. This breadth of approach is indispensable today; but it is comparatively new. More accurately, it is a recent renewal of a role of diplomacy that was important in the democracy of ancient Greece. In the days of Homer, and in the centuries following him, there were two kinds of envoys. One was a messenger, often sent in disguise, who carried a secret message to a king or military commander and brought back from him a secret reply. The other was a diplomat with a propagandistic function, who sought to appeal over the head of the ruler to create disaffection or to spread misrepresentations amongst his people.

In the *Iliad* Homer presents a scene in which the Greek orators appealed directly to the people of Troy, much as present-day Ambassadors utilize public meetings and television cameras. "But when before the Assembly of the Trojans," Homer wrote, "the Ambassadors began to weave the web of oratory and persuasion. Menelaus, although the younger of the two, spoke fluently, lucidly, and with few words—since he was not a garrulous man or one given to digressions. On the other hand, the resourceful Odysseus kept his eyes on the ground when he rose to speak, and held his staff rigidly in his hand, moving it neither to right nor to left, as if he were slow-witted. You would have taken him to be either sulky or stupid. But once you heard that great voice booming from his chest, and when the words fell one after the other like snowflakes on a winter's day, you realized that Odysseus, as an Ambassador, was beyond compare."

Similarly in his *History of the Peloponnesian Wars*, written some six hundred years after the fall of Troy, Thucydides represents the Ambassadors sent by Sparta to Athens as performing functions that seem startlingly modern. Sparta was plotting the conquest of Athens but wished to delay the conflict for a year or two while building its own strength and spreading disaffection among Athens' allies. An ambassadorial mission was sent to Athens with instructions to mingle freely and with great friendliness with the populace in order to "relax tensions" and try to keep the Athenians from proceeding with their own defensive armaments. The role of that mission could serve as a veritable model for the function of the Japanese Ambassador Nomura, in Washington, in 1941, or of such Communist spokesmen as Litvinov, Vishinsky, Chou En-lai, and Khrushchev.

When the rise of national states in Europe led to the re-establishment of diplomacy in the seventeenth century, an Ambassador could be slyly defined as "a man sent to lie abroad for his country." The diplomat became a "Minister Plenipotentiary," that is, a representative of his Monarch, with ample power to speak on behalf of the country he represented. In a time when a King could properly declare, "I am the State," it was useless for the Ambassador to direct his influence elsewhere than to the crown. Hence, diplomacy became a very personalized and extremely confidential business. Moreover, because of the slowness of communication, the Ambassador had to be authorized to conduct negotiations with a wide latitude of discretion. A typical example of a diplomatic mission in the style now known nostalgically as the "old diplomacy," is the group of Americans, headed by John Quincy Adams, who were sent to The Hague in 1813 to make the best peace terms they could with emissaries from Great Britain. Since three months were required for an exchange of views with Washington, the diplomats actually were "plenipotentiary"—empowered to exercise the authority of the executive branch of their Government. Their business was with Lord Castlereagh and the French Court. It never occurred to newspapermen to try to "cover" the day-by-day sessions; and the public, both in America and in Europe, knew nothing of what was happening until the treaty was ready to be signed.

Even as late as World War I, diplomacy was a closed profession. Diplomats were few in number, for not even England, France, and the United States maintained more than a dozen permanent missions abroad. Ambassadors were frock-coated gentlemen of great dignity, who spoke to one another and to few else. Woodrow Wilson startled this chaste community of professionals with his demand for "open covenants, openly arrived at." M. Jules Cambon, a skilled French practitioner of the old art, responded tartly: "The day secrecy is abolished, negotiation of any kind will become impossible." Newspaper reporters swarmed around the Conference of Versailles, and the world public clamored for news, but M. Cambon fought his own rear-guard action for the conduct of international affairs by trained professionals. "Expressions such as 'old diplomacy' and 'new diplomacy'," he wrote, "bear no relation to reality. It is the outward form—if you like, the 'adornments' of diplomacy—that are undergoing a change. The substance must remain the same, since human nature is unalterable; since there exists no other method of regulating international differences; and since the best instrument at the disposal of a Government wishing to persuade another Government will always remain the spoken words of a decent man."

In a way he was right. In the new day that he already saw on the horizon, the ways of diplomacy were to undergo great changes. Secrecy was to become virtually impossible; and the self-sufficient authority of emissaries has been dissipated now that they can receive daily or even hourly instructions from home. So level-headed a journalistic critic as C. L. Sulzberger, of the New York *Times,* can complain that "The postwar trend toward diplomacy by conference, diplomacy by loudspeaker, and diplomacy by insult has been hysterical." Walter Lippmann, too, has joined in denouncing the new diplomacy as "hoopla." But at least there remains what M. Cambon was sure cannot be dispensed with: spoken words. Indeed, far more words are used for a far vaster audience than ever before.

Aside from its secrecy and authority, the old diplomacy operated on a set of hypotheses that have very largely been abandoned in the past few years. First, it assumed that Europe was so far and away the center of world affairs that everything else was largely incidental. Secondly, it assumed that the important business of the earth was to be transacted solely amongst (and largely for the benefit of) a few Great Powers. Thirdly, is assumed that the Great Powers had responsibility over various spheres of influence and should be held accountable for what the minor nations in those areas might do. Fourthly, as a result of the foregoing considerations, the diplomatic corps was chiefly confined to a few European capitals, where (despite their national differences) they formed a club of professionals who shared similar tastes, sentiments, and background experiences. Today, of course, every one of these presumptions has either been dropped or persists as a vestigial obtruberance that hinders rather than helps the efficient operation of the international body politic.

The rapidity and completeness with which the world of diplomacy has been revolutionized is still difficult to comprehend. The new restrictions on their authority and the new conditions within which they must operate have resulted in a new breed of men in the diplomatic posts. Skill in making independent judgments has become of less importance than ability in teamwork and skill in presenting to varied audiences what others have formulated. In a sense, our diplomats have become less statesmen and more salesmen. As the functions of government (our own notably, but also those of other nations) have become more and more internationalized, the diplomatic functions are performed not alone by accredited representatives of the Department of State but also by agents of the Departments of Commerce, Treasury, Agriculture, Labor, and a bevy of independent agencies. Globe-trotting Congressmen and Senators have become diplomats in effect. So, to a degree, are important news-reporters, educators, and businessmen. Even casual and wholly untutored tourists are quite properly described as "unofficial diplomats." So too are the movies and books, the magazines, plays, and music which find their way abroad. In still another sense, even the events and conditions within the country play a vital "representative" role abroad—as is well illustrated by world-wide interest in the racial situation of the United States and the Union of South Africa.

It is easy to sympathize with the complaint of traditional diplomats that this kind of broadening of the meaning of diplomacy is tantamount to destroying the concept. It can readily be argued that no one is truly a diplomat except one of the hundred-odd individuals who have been vested with "plenipotentiary status" by the

Department of State and approved in this role by the Senate. On occasion it is valuable to remember that what is said by a Congressman or a businessman or a demagogue in some local community is not in fact the official policy of the Government. Nevertheless, it is also important to keep in mind that diplomacy depends upon the field of international communication; and communication nowadays flows from multiple sources and expresses itself in innumerable ways.

In still another way has the function of the old style diplomat been drastically altered. In prior times he indubitably represented only and strictly his own Government. Alliances were, of course, important and often were broad enough in scope to encompass many aspects of national action. But today alliances have become so vastly important as to all but dwarf national individuality. The Arab-Asian Bloc in the United Nations, for example, is a powerful entity that speaks for twenty-five or so member States. Powerful as the United States is, we nonetheless speak often in terms of the Free World or the democracies. The United States cannot by itself make or exercise or state a policy toward Cuba without regard for our Allies, any more than France and England could toward Suez. A modern diplomat, understandably, cannot be quite sure who or what he represents.

If the examples cited may be swept away with the exclamation, "After all, every nation is committed to its own self-interest and surely every diplomat is sworn to represent truly and dependably his own sovereign," the answer may be that this is literally true; but the examples are not the less significant. Independence among nations has been gradually but actually transmuted into significant interdependence. In the same vein, but less disputably, our diplomats no longer can speak solely for their own Department of State or Foreign Office; they must correlate their positions with those taken by a whole host of other governmental offices. Conferences —international and inter-departmental—have become increasingly indispensable as the means of formulating policies. One of the principal problems diplomacy represents is that this correlation of views has not yet proceeded far enough to be dependable. Contradictory statements by various spokesmen, that have to be explained away, are frequent occurrences.

Internationalism has become a fetish—precisely at the same time in history in which extreme and exuberant nationalism is flourishing as never before in world history. "The American people are now life members of the world community and they know it," Carroll Binder of the Minneapolis *Tribune* could say to a meeting of the American Philosophical Society (in 1948). But he had to add quickly "—even if they do not know how to exercise that membership." E. S. Glenn, in a State Department release in 1955, asked rhetorically, "What is a world view?" and answered with professorial precision: "A manner of conceiving the universe of human preoccupations and of forming, ordering, and relating the different subdivisions thereof." It looks like a good statement —for a class in political science. Our diplomats are desperately in need of a world view; but they lack the knowledge and as yet lack the authorization for forming, ordering, or relating their activities in any such context.

At the Foreign Ministers Conference in Geneva, in November, 1955, M. Antoine Pinay of France attempted to spell out the requirements of the new diplomacy, at least insofar as they apply to official diplomats at international conferences:

> Too often, in the past, the exchanges of views in which representatives of our governments participated were transformed into platforms—from whose height each addressed the public opinion of the others.
>
> Too often our discussions have been only an interminable alternation of successive monologues.
>
> We ought, first of all, to bend all our efforts to resist the temptation—all too natural and all too easy—to make long speeches.
>
> A conference is not a series of closed monologues, where each side simply stays within its own viewpoint and remains deaf to the viewpoint of the others.
>
> It ought to be a series of dialogues, where the human contact which allows one man to put himself in the place of the other, and to understand the other, can be established and maintained.

There is no real progress without mutual comprehension.
Let us try, then, sir, to recover this spirit of dialogue we have
lost to some extent.

Like his earlier compatriot, M. Cambon, whom we have quoted
earlier, M. Pinay appears to represent more a nostalgic wistfullness
for a vanished past than a realistic hope for the future. Diplomacy
has abandoned the striped trousers and frock coats of the era of
mysteriously secretive professionals. Professionalism, of course, is
no less needed than before; but what is now demanded above all
is skill in debate and in propaganda. The closed conference room
has been succeeded by the mass audience. Appeals must be directed
not to sophisticated compeers, but to the men and women who
work the fields and the factories, the rice paddies and the mines, of
all the world. Of course, much that diplomats say is still said to
one another—and some of it behind closed doors. But more and
more, the major appeal is now to public opinion, both at home and
abroad.

The importance of domestic public opinion in the formulation and carrying out of foreign policy, and also the way a very
skilled professional dealt with it, may be illustrated by describing
how President Franklin D. Roosevelt set about introducing his
program of Lend-Lease Aid for England and her Allies in 1941.
Dunkirk had fallen, all of Europe from the Pyrenees to northern
Norway was in Hitler's hands, and England was suffering from a
rain of Nazi bombs on her defenseless cities. The American people
were concerned but not aroused. Polls taken in July, 1940, showed
that one fourth of Americans thought it more important to keep
out of the war than to help England; one-third felt it important to
help England even at the risk of war; the remaining two-fifths
wanted to avoid all risk of entering the war but felt "something"
should be done to help England. At about this same time a poll
taken at the University of Michigan showed that 80% of the students opposed entrance of the United States into the war even if
this should be the only way to prevent the complete defeat of
England and France. This was the state of public opinion which
President Roosevelt pondered while he had his staff working on
fifty successive drafts of a highly secret bill to give substantial aid

to our European Allies. Finally, he worked out his strategy and commenced a campaign to shift public opinion into a more favorable climate.

On December 17, 1940, at a press conference, he casually answered a question about our policy toward the war by saying that, "If my neighbor's house should catch fire, I would surely lend him my garden hose." In a Fireside Chat on Sunday evening, December 29, he declared that America's function was not to fight in the war but to be the Arsenal of Democracy. A week later, on January 6, 1941, he presented his State of the Union address to Congress, incorporating in it his theme that there are "Four Freedoms" which must be defended—freedom of speech and religion, and freedom from want and fear. Meanwhile, on January 3, he had deliberately aroused widespread speculation by sending Harry Hopkins on a confidential mission to London; but despite eleven questions asked him by the press, he persisted in saying (laughingly) that the mission had no significance except to carry his personal greetings to Churchill. Of course he expected to arouse considerable speculation on what was really intended. Finally, on January 16, after this careful period of preparation, he presented the Lend-Lease bill for consideration by the Congress. Even then, in successive weekly polls taken through March 8, the percentage of public opinion favoring the bill did not rise above 58%. Without his preparatory efforts, we may assume the bill would not have passed.

Even under so absolute a dictatorship as that established by Adolf Hitler in Nazi Germany, his principal aide, Herman Goering, in 1934 stressed to a party gathering the urgent need for continuous efforts to strengthen and maintain public support for the policies of the regime. Said Goering:

> Anyone today who thinks that, because we have the power of the State, the propagandists of the Movement need no longer carry on their work shows a complete failure to understand the nature and requirements of modern propaganda and public enlightenment.

He went on to portray the stupendous efforts of nationwide propaganda that had been necessary to bring the Nazis into power and warned that if the effort should be relaxed the movement could not succeed.

The chief concern of our diplomats, nevertheless, is with public opinion abroad. Notoriously, Soviet Russia far surpasses our efforts in this field. What Russia spends and how are secrets not easily penetrated; but F. Bowen Evans, author of a careful book on *Worldwide Communist Propaganda Activities* (1955), estimates it at more than three billion dollars annually. The United States established the Voice of America in 1948 and has since then spent from eleven to some seventy-five millions of dollars annually on it and related "information" programs—an annual sum equal to the cost of fighting from one to seven minutes of World War II. England spends perhaps four times as much on international broadcasting.

No nation, either communistic or democratic, seeks to influence public opinion as a whole. Russia selects as "target audiences" our college campuses, intellectuals, labor unions, and minority groups. The United States seeks to aim its messages in various countries at specific groups which we feel are open to persuasion and also at least potentially able to influence their governmental policies. In any nation, the people whose opinions can be influenced must be those who can be reached. For example, our motion pictures are shown in every part of the world—but in Asia there is a cinema seat for only one in 300 of the population; in Africa, for one in 210; in South America, one for each 35; and in Europe one for every 26 people. Television programs can be telecast into some sixty million American homes but only half a million in Japan and some 600,000 in Australia.

In 1950 UNESCO undertook the first global survey to determine the relative availability of information in various countries. In its latest study of this sort, released in May, 1961, it found that in the United States for every 1,000 people, 327 newspapers are printed daily; in Great Britain, 573. Interestingly, in Tokyo and Osaka, every Japanese family daily received two or more newspapers. In Russia there are 161 newspapers for every 1,000 inhabitants; but in Africa, only one newspaper for every 192 people.

Since most international propaganda is disseminated by radio, the information on distribution of radio receivers is especially significant. There are some 160,000,000 radio sets in the world, or one for every 15 people. In the United States there are 566 per 1,000 people; in Sweden, 298 per 1,000; in Canada, 237 per 1,000; in Great Britain 227, per 1,000; in Russia, 40 per 1,000; in India 7 per 1,000; and in China, 2 per 1,000. Of ten and a half million radio sets in the Far East, eight million are in Japan. The United States has a radio for every two people; Ethiopia one for each 2,000. Obviously, some areas are far more "open" than are others to verbal propaganda. Perhaps Russia is more successful than we seem to be in many "under-developed" areas because of its greater efforts to send in individuals to carry on person-to-person propaganda work.

Who, then, are the diplomats? Who is it who creates the images abroad which peoples (and even governments) gradually build up of our nation and of others? When diplomacy is viewed in this manner, it becomes obvious that the diplomats are not confined to official stations. They are motion pictures and newspapers. They are businessmen and tourists. They are race riots and space satellites. They are whatever happens—whatever is said about what happens—and much that is not said. We may call this the "new" diplomacy; or we may call it "total" diplomacy. We may regret its lack of discipline, its disorderliness and contradictions, its harmful revelation of much that would be better kept concealed. But we scarcely can ignore the fact that it exists.

The question remains—and is becoming acute—of how we may better prepare ourselves to fight the battle of opinion, the war for the minds of men, which is being waged with increasing intensity and ever more broadly. In the chapters that follow, these are the questions that will be explored.

Chapter 3

SPEECH: THE LIFE OF A DIPLOMAT

BEN C. LIMB

WHAT DOES A diplomat do? Well—for one thing, he makes speeches. He also writes philosophical interpretations of governmental theory for scholarly quarterlies, factual analyses of trade and production data for economic weeklies, tender and pathetic accounts of courage among the war refugees (and what diplomat lacks them in these times?) for the house organs of the great charitable organizations, commentaries on the equipoise of military power as it affects his country for some of the numerous magazines specializing in ground or sea or air warfare, and forecasts concerning domestic and international politics for the elite monthlies. And he does not overlook occasional brief pieces for such special periodicals as those issued by boys' clubs, milk dealers, aluminum manufacturers, and the association of tobacco auctioneers.

And when he isn't writing, he speaks. He speaks at formal assemblies of the United Nations and at special international conferences to which his Government may appoint him a delegate. He speaks informally to small delegations that visit his office to present a gift, a petition, or a resolution of commendation on some stand recently taken by his Government. He speaks to women's clubs, to men's service luncheons, to colleges and to grade schools, to the annual banquets of labor unions and bankers, to community forums which have question periods, and on radio and television discussion panels where he is the bull's-eye in a target aimed at by several of "the nation's leading news analysts." He speaks to boys' clubs and to girls' clubs, to church groups and to investors' syndicates, to county fairs and to select dinner meetings of leading financiers. He talks to Congressmen, and State Department officials, and other Ambassadors, and Executive-Secretaries of organizations ranging from Infuriated Taxpayers Arrayed Against Foreign Aid to Aroused Citizens Militantly Marshalled to Defend International Democracy.

For several hours each day he sits at his desk writing letters. He writes to learned professors whose lifetime specialty is the inter-relationship of the vowel system of his national language with that of the Seminole Indians, and to returned servicemen who want to know the name and address of an orphan-child photographed with a big smile while receiving a can of GI rations on a cold street corner during the terrible winter retreat. He writes to lonely and warmhearted couples who would like to adopt a child from his country, and to business opportunists who think his people ought to provide an ideal market for a newly invented gadget. He writes to the Den Mother of Cub Scouts in a South Dakota village who wants a list of eleven grade-school children in his country who can and wish to correspond with her charges (in the English language). And he writes scores of thank-you letters to the many people who express admiration for the courage of his countrymen in resisting aggression.

He also dines. He attends formal dinners given by other am-bassadors on the occasion of their national holidays. (Every one of the hundred-odd nations has at least two or three holidays which merit attendance by top-ranking representatives of all the nations with which they have friendly relations.) He attends special lunch-eons which feature the unique dishes of various countries or of regional or cultural groups in the United States. He goes to cocktail parties and afternoon teas. He goes on picnics and excursions. He accepts invitations for breakfasts and for midnight snacks. And be-tween times he follows a rigorous diet to keep his weight from be-coming more than he can carry around.

And he travels! His secretary keeps on file the schedules of air-lines, trains, buses, and ferryboats (with notations of deviations from the schedule on Sundays and holidays). He is in New Eng-land for a meeting one evening, and in Illinois (on the way to California) for another meeting the next day. He dashes through traffic in Washington and New York, and flies above storm clouds over Minnesota. And he carries a portable dictaphone so he can keep up with his correspondence while en route.

Between times he works on incoming and outgoing reports, conducts conferences, makes lavish use of the telephone, and studies endless reams of data in connection with projects assigned to him by his Government. He reads an assortment of ministerial reports and of daily newspapers from his own country, to keep up to date on what is happening and on the tenor of opinion of his own folks back home; and he reads even more newspapers of the country to which he is accredited so that he can send back summary reports of opinion for the guidance of his own Government. He administers his own staff, and he worries about the inadequacies of his own office budget.

Finally—and by no means least important—he studies. His desk is surrounded by almanacs, dictionaries, encyclopedias, histories, a selection of new books, and standard reference works. He tries not to be ignorant of cultural developments in his own country in the twelfth century or of the possible influence of new industrial techniques in affecting production of basic commodities important for his nation's trade or domestic consumption. He knows that at any moment he may be asked for an opinion concerning a little-known writer of his own homeland or about a foreign commentary on his country's political developments. He will be expected to know the status of the religious development, the figures on coal-mining, the adequacy of technological training programs, and the problems of commercial fishing in his homeland. The questions sometimes will reveal an appalling ignorance which requires of him a background lecture to set the facts in perspective; and sometimes he will be queried by an expert who has just completed a scholarly treatise on some obscure facet of his national dramaturgy.

With such a program, the serious question arises as to how an ambassador lives. If he is not a bachelor, he has a wife and perhaps several children whom he loves and with whom he would like to have a certain amount of normal family life. The chances are that his children are sent away to boarding schools, where they will be relieved of the daily disappointments of home appointments broken by the demands of official duties. His wife either retreats into a lonely world of her own, or adapts herself to a round of continuously unexpected visitors and visiting. The family medicine chest accumulates a huge collection of cures for indigestion and insomnia. Since ambassadorial salaries are not large, serious family discussions are held on the clothing budget, the servant problem, and how to devise cheaper vacations. And since the ambassador (and his wife) must always be poised, pleasant, and alert in public, he (and she) very likely will be moody, irritable, and occasionally depressed in the privacy of their apartment.

Diplomacy is a mad profession. But that madness is madness with a system. Wherever he goes and whatever he does, the ambassador is the titular representative of his Government. While on duty (and he is always on duty) he is the alter ego abroad of his President. Whatever he says is official governmental policy. How he comports himself determines to a large degree the attitude of the people he meets toward his own people at home. Nor can he escape from the difficulties by saying nothing, for "no comment" on crucial issues (and what issue is not crucial these days to some segment or other of the public or of officialdom?) can often be more devastating than even a fumbled malapropism.

It follows, then, that diplomacy is above all a profession of words—written and spoken. Diplomacy should be listed among the categories of the literary and oratorical professions—somewhere midway between the serious essayists and the lyric poets, or between the commemorative orators and the after-dinner speakers. And still another sublisting should be entered under Conversation: Formal and Informal. Above all, and in multitudinous ways, the diplomat is a man of words.

He talks—and he also listens. He listens with dubious caution to earnest crusaders who seek him out to pour into his ears detailed suggestions of what they consider brilliant solutions for what they are certain are fundamental problems confronting his country. He listens with agreeable pleasure to complicated jokes—which may not be as fresh to him as they are to the narrator. He listens with educated discrimination to discussions of aesthetic influences upon the art and literature of his nation. He listens with perceptive acuity to veiled hints of policies not yet ready for public announcement—and many of which are pure fabrications of the diplomatic rumor factory. He listens to comments on international affairs heard in snatches in elevators, in restaurants, and on street corners —and tries to estimate to what extent they may represent widespread public opinion. He listens to the words of guests who have been invited so that they may meet in person the "distinguished ambassador"—or "that man who has been making all those terrible statements."

Yes, he listens, he studies, he confers. And then (frequently after midnight) he goes into his study and prepares what he shall say the next day. And at this point he becomes a literary figure with a difference. For oftentimes his main concern is not to set down in clear and simple language a statement of facts so obvious that it cannot be misunderstood (which I believe is one of the hallmarks of great writing). Quite to the contrary, his purpose often is to concoct an ambiguous composition which—no matter how carefully it may be analyzed—will add up to no real meaning whatsoever.

One of the distressing themes of which editorial writers are fond is a ringing plea that diplomats should try to master the art of plain and straight-forward talk. This theme is peculiarly distressing to diplomats, for it represents a basic misunderstanding of one of their greatest contributions to humanity.

Diplomats (to use a somewhat strained analogy) are grease on the wheels of a Rube Goldbergian machine of disconnected and clashing international machinery. The clearest and most simple fact of international affairs is that they are, indeed, *inter*-national. Governments are instituted to serve their own people; and every Government has a people of its own to serve. Each Government aims at the achievement of its own purposes—and sometimes these purposes clash.

Disputes between and among governments are far from uncommon, even when the relationships of the peoples involved are basically friendly and cooperative. Differences exist on all manner of policies—ranging from the recognition of Red China to the interpretation of fisheries rights on the open seas. There are varying problems and points of view on the timing of policies that are in agreement, and on the wording of minor clauses in major documents. There are disputes on questions which are imbedded in the domestic politics of one or all the nations concerned. There are disputes which could lead to temporary irritation and there are disputes which could result in war.

The diplomat, let it never be forgotten, represents a sovereign nation. And there are no nations which are not sovereign. There are treaties and alliances which represent temporary and partial surrenders of some modicum of sovereignty. There is the United Nations, where over a hundred nations meet at council tables to talk about questions of common interest. There is a growing climate of internationalism and a growing sense of global inter-dependency. There are trans-national influences, such as religion and trade. But there remain separate governments, each, as Mark Twain might have said, with its own fish to fry.

And in the midst of this clashing dissonance of diverse purposes and methods there stands the little group of ambassadors busily (and necessarily) applying the lubricant of ambiguity.

All of the people (and their name is legion) who deliver themselves periodically of lectures to the diplomatic corps on the presumed virtues of plain speaking should be sent back to school. And when they are settled down as a captive audience in a classroom, some dispassionate professor should lecture to them, with a host of specific examples, on what the results would be if all diplomats should always express clearly and forthrightly precisely what their own governments believed and desired.

As a specific instance (and these are always dangerous!) what should be the reply of an "under-developed" nation's ambassador to a question asked in a public forum about some phase of the administration of American aid funds with which his Government happened to be seriously displeased? Should he describe clearly just what it is in the program that his Government dislikes—and thereby risk arousing resentment and perhaps contribute ammunition to a minority group that wants to end all foreign aid? Or, on the other hand, should he clearly and unmistakably endorse the entire program (in order to win support for it), thereby undermining the efforts of his Government to secure some revisions? Obviously, it seems to me, he should do neither. On the contrary, he should deliver himself of sentiments which will seem to be sufficiently explicit to satisfy the questioner, but in such circumlocutions that the sentiments expressed could not possibly be understood.

The real purpose of such ambiguities is to mask and minimize disagreements while experts are hard at work behind the scenes trying to eliminate their causes. So long as the separate sovereignty of nations is preserved, this will inevitably be a considerable part of the diplomat's job. It simply cannot be otherwise. When an occasional inexperienced or unskilled diplomat overlooks this essential fact, the consequences are immediate, most unpleasant, and often serious. Later explanations never quite catch up with the original *faux pas*.

The serious study of diplomatic speech is still, unfortunately, in its infancy, Diplomats perforce must hammer out their own rules in the midst of their day-by-day duties. Experience has to be interpreted rapidly, for the conditions and even the rules of international conferences are constantly changing.

Just a few years ago diplomacy was conducted by leisurely gentlemen who wore striped trousers and morning coats and sat in impressive offices conducting infrequent and genteel conversations. Occasional written communications (often handwritten by the ambassador himself) were exchanged between governments whose affairs seldom interlocked. As for public appearances, the old-time diplomat (and not so old as we might think) was expected to do no more than deliver polite and inconsequential after-dinner speeches composed chiefly of refurbished jokes. When international conferences were held, they were behind locked doors and the public did not expect ever to hear any more about them than the conclusions finally formulated into policies.

The global telegraphic network, radio, the movie news camera, the airplane, and television have wrought changes that are still occurring at a dizzy pace. Nowadays, "closed conferences" are about as open as a community sewing bee. Everything that is said, how it is said, and who says it are known to all who are interested within a few minutes or hours. Moreover, diplomats nowadays talk not only to one another, but to the public in the nation to which they are accredited. And the accumulation of all the instantaneous information that is now available, plus the sense of world community created by modern transportation and communication, has aroused an interest in practically anything that happens anywhere. Diplomacy in our time is conducted on an open stage.

It should not be assumed, however, that a diplomat must always be ambiguous. Occasions also frequently arise when what he must strive for above all else is to secure a clear and correct understanding of a governmental policy or of conditions within his own country. And this, too, presents problems.

For example, a delegation of labor-liberals may visit his country and upon their return may secure wide publicity for views critical of the working conditions which they observed. They, of course, are not experts on the conditions in the country they have visited. And what they have to say is addressed primarily to their own home constituency, to impress upon their followers and their own Congressmen the sincerity of their determination to achieve "good" conditions for workmen. So far so good.

However, an incidental result of their publicized criticism is a lessening of respect and friendship for the nation which they have criticized. Often the facts they cite may be correct in themselves, but are decidedly out of focus in terms of the general economic, social, and political conditions within which those facts must necessarily exist. Long working hours, for instance, have always been inseparably connected with lack of machines. Low wages are correlated with low prices. Just as in the United States, advances in labor conditions have to be related to general advances of technology. The slow process of education is required to train an expert body of technicians. Laws have to be revised by legislatures which are subject to periodic election campaigns. Money has to be found for investment in new modes of productivity. Bad conditions do not exist because anyone desires them, but are inherent in complicated situations that require widespread and often gradual remedial action. All of this needs to be explained.

And it needs to be explained to a public that will read a headline charging that the work-week is too long, but will not read a three-thousand word article explaining why. Notoriously, it is easy to criticize and difficult to educate.

The foreign correspondents of American newspapers face this same problem when they seek to write dispatches on complicated political situations (and politics are always complicated). They seek to escape from their dilemma by using catch-phrases, such as "rightist," "liberal," and "leftist," which their readers will understand, but which often only dimly if at all reflect the actual conditions they are supposed to explain. Under these circumstances, the ambassador is always goaded by his own sense of righteousness and by urgent messages from his home Government to "rectify" the misunderstandings.

In one sense, at least, the plight of the diplomat is akin to that of the public school teacher who heroically attempts to explain Einstein's quantum theory in simple terms that will be understandable to grade-school pupils. At least the teacher has a captive audience that has to listen and try to understand.

The diplomat, faced with this problem, seeks to phrase his own understanding of the essential facts in terms that will reflect conditions in his homeland accurately and at the same time will be interesting and understandable to the public of the nation to which he is accredited. He wracks his brain for a headline phrase which will be as instantly appealing as that used by his country's critics. And such phrases, under the circumstances, are not easily come by.

Now, it may seem that the diplomat faces an impossibly difficult job. Maybe so. It is certainly difficult enough so that no ambassador in his right mind expects to be more than partially and occasionally successful. But there also are rewards and compensations. The anterooms of national executives are seldom crowded with diplomats who are pleading to be relieved of their posts. On the contrary, most ambassadors appear to enjoy their jobs and are generally reluctant to leave them. Diplomacy, like printer's ink, gets in the blood and keeps the true professional devotedly at his tasks.

Perhaps the major appeal of the diplomatic profession is the sense it gives (partly correctly) that the ambassador is behind the scenes and on the inside in the unfolding of the great world drama of human affairs.

To a degree never before known, the ordinary lives of ordinary people are dependent upon international relations. Hot war, cold war, psychological warfare, trade, tourism, and many facets of daily living are interwoven with the relationships of nations. What decisions are made, and a portion of the processes by which these decisions are reached, are public property. Every citizen can see pictures of the great statesmen meeting together, and can read "dope" stories by skilled news analysts on how their personalities interact.

But the diplomats, nevertheless, are a special club—a group set apart. They, and only they, can assess accurately the degree to which policies are affected by personalities and, sometimes, by sheer accidents. They can appreciate one another's difficulties in phrasing statements and in dealing with public reactions. They naturally develop a "clubbable" atmosphere among themselves. They know which diplomats violate the unbreakable rules of behavior, and which ones, with skill and ofttimes personal sacrifice, keep the gears from clashing unmercifully. In their own cocktail parties and private luncheons, they (like everyone else) often let down their hair and talk shop. And this helps them keep their perspective and balance.

What should we say to a young man or young woman who would like to get into the diplomatic service? The best advice is— don't! But if you must, start young and learn everything you possibly can: about your own country, about the world at large, present and past. Study languages, and above all study human nature. Learn to say what you mean—both so it can't be understood and so it couldn't possibly be misunderstood by anyone. Develop poise and ease in all social circumstances, under all manner of unmannerly provocations. Be interested in everyone and in everything.

More seriously, diplomacy is a profession for those who not only have the skills required but above all else have a dedicated sense of public service. The great problem of our age is how to restore justice in world affairs without the cost of war. The great need is to find some way of solving problems which in the past decade have largely been postponed. What humanity desperately needs is diplomats who will stand with courage for the ideals which represent the best in civilization—and will find a way of accomplishing them peacefully if possible.

The diplomat is far indeed from being the dilettante who

specializes in personal charm. He is the instrument of humanity, charged with the successful achievement of tenable solutions to the issues of life and death. If he fails, the human race may fail. It is not a profession to be taken lightly, either by those who practice it or by those who dimly and distantly observe. It is this sense of mission which keeps the real diplomats—the representatives of free people—unwearyingly at their tasks.

Chapter 4

SPEECH AND DIPLOMACY

R. Smith Simpson

Those of us dealing with international developments have especial reason to appreciate how essential is skill and prudence in speech, for an utterance of international interest has a trajectory of an awe-inspiring scale. Just let some piece of nonsense issue from a human muzzle and off it goes, like an unguided missile, on a tingling journey to the furthermost corners of the earth, working a withering havoc before settling to earth, one knows not where. In its course, it sets up equally tingling reactions, startling long-dormant opinions, prejudices and emotions, until sometimes one hardly knows where or how to begin to grapple with its effects.

Not only that. It is remarkable how often the observation of an individual—even a private individual—acquires an attribution to an entire nation. When this occurs, it can set back months of patient, heart-searching effort to promote sensible relations between that individual's nation and another. Armed with the means of becoming the printed word, the spoken word of the twentieth century can travel a long way from home, with lightning swiftness, its destruction to perform.

At the same time that some piece of nonsense is taking flight and magically acquiring, so soon as it passes a national boundary, the great elevated character of a national opinion, some remark of commonsense is having difficulty even getting off the ground. That remark may be independent or it may be intended as a chaser of the nonsensical. In either case, it seldom acquires the fast sweep of the ridiculous. A sober thought, like a sober man, seems to be less newsworthy than its opposite.

It is for this reason that some participants in international relations have turned for consolation to a more distant, less disconcerting age when international relations were conducted if not by clicks and grunts, at least by measured words. Such was the age of Louis XIV, when foreign policy was the prerogative of monarchs and diplomats and not encroached upon by the chatter of the multitude. This is the age Sir Harold Nicolson esteems.

In his latest reflections on diplomacy, *The Evolution of Diplomatic Method,* Sir Harold has taken the present age severely to task for substituting a blatant "forensic propaganda" for the reasonable, quiet, and proven methods of diplomacy by the diplomats. While not proposing to scrap all existing machinery and return to the eighteenth or nineteenth centuries, he nevertheless is of the view that from the advent of Richelieu to power in 1616 until revolution began to rumble 160 years later, France achieved a perfection of the diplomatic method never achieved before or since by any other nation. But with his usual acumen, Sir Harold qualifies his praise of that method. The *caveat* he enters is that *"given the ideas and circumstances of the time, it was an excellent method."*

That seems to be a prudent qualification and I have italicized it for the emphasis I believe it deserves. One can judge methods and ideas only in the context of their time. It therefore seems wise that, instead of roundly condemning the furore which characterizes much of the world's international relations in the mid-twentieth century, one should analyze the *methods* of our time and the *conditions* of our time, in search of suitable criteria for evaluating our efficacy and weakness in the field of diplomacy. Thence one may proceed to a consideration of means of improvement.

This is too large a project for a single chapter, and I will limit myself to analyzing one sector only of the methods of diplomacy in our present age, namely the role and methods of speech employed by the diplomatist. Examined with the large background in mind, this limited subject may prove to be one of genuine interest.

Ever since man began to communicate, oral communication has been deemed more persuasive than written. Thus, diplomacy, from its own primitive beginnings, has relied primarily upon speech. This has been true not only in the conduct of negotiations but also in the preparation for missions and in the justification of their results.

Permanent, continuous diplomatic service is of fairly recent origin. In ancient times, ambassadors were designated for specific, immediate objectives and when these were attained or it became obvious they could not be attained, the diplomatic appointment came to an end. The employment was *ad hoc* and generally a matter of months. It was usually limited to negotiation. Very often, in the Greek city states, the mission was concluded by a debate in a popular assembly. So speech has had a very ancient emphasis not only in the conduct but in the review of diplomacy.

It was not until Italian city states came to appreciate in the late Middle Ages the importance of systematic communication with other governments that ambassadors and their retinues acquired permanent residence in foreign capitals. This importance once realized, ambassadors and their assistants swiftly made their mark as indispensable tools in the accomplishment of inter-governmental objectives. They not only proved acute observers of political and economic conditions in the states to which they were sent, but they were residents of those states for long enough periods to permit their acuteness to ripen into understanding.

Intelligence is one thing; understanding is another; and the Italian city states were wise enough to assure themselves of both. So true was this, in fact, that the detailed reports of the Venetian diplomats constitute a prime source of historical knowledge of their times. They had no popular assemblies, however, to which they were obliged to account and diplomacy settled into the grooves of the conversational and the written word.

It was thus that the diplomatist acquired his repute as a good conversationalist. Conducting his business with monarchs and ministers, he acquired a mastery of the polite phrase, the *bon mot*, the witty repartee, which became his stock in trade. In accordance with forms established by custom, diplomatic intercourse became confined largely to informal communication, oral and written, and to formal notes, memoranda and despatches.

With the clattering rise of moveable type and the printing press came the spread of representative assemblies and when the chatter of the telegrapher's key was added to this growing rattle of reporting and opinion on international developments, the diplomatic fraternity began to realize that a steadily expanding range of affairs was intruding upon their polite and serene existence. Diplomacy then began to swing into an arc subtending a considerably wider angle of affairs. With this came the necessity of expanding and developing diplomatic techniques, some of which had become of specialized employment only. One of these was the art of oral communication. In proportion as the diplomatic guild failed to appreciate this growing democratization of international affairs and adjusted to it, it drew the ridicule of the democratic age, traces of which can still be found in this second half of the twentieth century.

The result of all these changes is that nowadays the uses to which the diplomatist puts oral communication are exceedingly varied. Let us consider the case of an American citizen who has been appointed to an ambassadorship.

Before departing on his mission, the appointee must review his assignment with appropriate officials in the State Department. Whether he be a career diplomat or a political appointee, he and the Department must get their lines straight. Since, unlike his ancient prototype, the modern ambassador is no longer dispatched for a single objective to be attained through a single negotiation, but is to be gone for some time, he must keep in mind a whole range of problems, methods and relationships. Nor do these concern simply the country to which he is assigned. The interdependence of countries is such that many are often concerned with the policies affecting one. Hence, moves require an awareness of a whole series of repercussions, which may develop with the chain-like rapidity of a disintegrating atom.

The diplomatist who knows what he is about and can express himself adequately has shown that, in this process of establishing a "meeting of the minds" with the Department, he need not be a mere agent of his government: he can do much to influence the definition and clarification of objectives and methods and the emphases to be distributed among them. What a diplomatist is and what influence he exerts depends a good deal on the diplomatist and it is as evident in this phase of his career as in any other.

International relations interweave so wide a variety of interests and objectives these days that a ministry of foreign affairs is hard put to it to interlace and reconcile these in a manner to avoid contradictions and achieve the strength and respect which comes from a unity of purpose. Much grist for this mill of coordination is provided by such Departments as those of Commerce, Labor, Agriculture, Treasury and Defense, to mention a few, as well as by independent agencies of the Government. Other departments and agencies than the State Department must therefore be drawn into the process of an American diplomatist's preparation for his mission, which is concluded by a conference with the President. All this consultation is conducted orally.

Once at his post, the diplomatist's consultations begin with his staff and focus upon his immediate operational requirements. He needs "filling in" on the condition of his staff, which is always in a state of some flux, due to transfers, leaves, illness or the Department's inability to come up with a needed person at a particular time. This "filling in" began in Washington and is carried a step further on his arrival at post and proceeds thereafter as a never-ending development by which the diplomatist seeks the most effective staff possible. The ambassador needs "filling in" on the government to which he is assigned and those officials whom he will be shortly meeting, once his credentials have been presented. He needs "filling in" on conditions in the country itself, so that even his earliest approaches to the government will evidence the best possible grasp of the realities into which our policies must be dovetailed.

Such consultations involve a good deal of "give and take" between an ambassador and his staff. In these staff conferences, each officer is provided the opportunity of communicating to others and acquiring for himself a broader basis of fact and perspective than he can possibly obtain alone. Two heads are better than one, no matter how good one may be. Hence, an open mind never fails to be enriched by these exchanges, and this goes for the diplomatist of experience as well as for the novitiate.

Having just benefitted from a review of things in Washington, the chief of a mission can supply not only the latest information from the capital but an insight into Washington's thinking from all the various angles of its many-sided prism of policy. It is interesting to one of some years of foreign service to observe and compare the variety in the quality of such presentations by a newly-arrived chief. Here is a point at which perceptiveness and articulation come fully into play and can do much to determine the efficacy of a mission in its many functions.

One might dilate a little on staff meetings, for they illustrate one of the more distinct departures from the diplomacy of a period no more remote than fifty years ago and the new importance which oral presentation has acquired among all ranks of those who participate in the diplomatic process. When missions are small, ambassadors can carry most things in their own heads and when they consult their staff they do so on an individual basis—sometimes, we are informed by memoirs, in so informal a way as on a stroll through a park. But with the growing complexity of international relationships and rapidity of communication, no single ambassador can successfully carry all the more important things in his head. He must necessarily work with a large number of associates ranking from a counsellor—or several counsellors—on down through first, second and third secretaries, as well as military and other specialized attaches. Hence, staff meetings have became an accepted part of a mission's regime and the degree of success with which they are conducted does much to determine the mission's effectiveness.

Human nature being what it is, the courage to present a dissent from a prevailing view is not entirely universal. An officer who wants to get ahead rapidly may decide to play things safe and "go along" with prevailing views rather than to speak out against them. How one conducts himself, I suppose, depends largely on how one views his position—whether as a vehicle of his own career or as a means of service to his country and the great causes to which he considers it committed. There are many times when this distinction is a real one and an officer is put to the acid test—a test all the more difficult since he is far from home base and lacks the means of a civil servant in the capital to keep his lines straight and assure that all interested parties are informed exactly as to what he has in mind and why he is opposing a popular policy.

Given the independence to think for himself and the courage to speak up, an officer needs to consider carefully not only what his differing viewpoint is but also how best to present it. Staff meetings can be quite sizeable these days, thereby requiring of those participating in them an effective faculty in oral presentation. Good sense and tact are essential elements, for the purpose of offering a dissenting view is not to provide an exercise in disagreement but to make that view acceptable to others. One is trying to induce a majority to pause in one course, perhaps a well-grooved course, long enough to weigh the merits of quite a different course. That is not easy. There is an intellectual momentum, as well as a physical momentum, that travels with the sheer weight of numbers and it is sometimes startling to see how this can be so even in a gathering of intelligent people. It can at times be a little awe-inspiring.

In considering his approach to any situation such as this, an officer must consider, as I say, not only the substance of what he feels compelled to present, but the manner in which to present it. And here the person who has had some discipline in oral presentation finds himself advantageously situated. He knows he must watch even the tone of his voice. One sometimes witnesses a good case spoiled in a staff meeting by nothing more than an unfortunate tone employed in its presentation.

Once installed in his mission and his credentials presented, an ambassador extends the range of his consultation to the officials of the accrediting government and to private citizens. A good deal of circumspection is needed in this process. Not only is there a protocol to be observed in going at a government, but common sense and tact; and as far as private citizens are concerned, mistakes of judgment as to whom the diplomatist sees first can be distinctly unhelpful. The diplomatist's first moves will naturally be observed with interest by the government to which he is accredited, and none more than his approaches to private individuals whom he judges important to consult first. Prudence dictates the greatest discretion in this, in order to avoid misunderstandings of intentions and emphases, and the advice of a mission's staff is wisely drawn upon in the selection and timing of such consultations.

His assignment under way, the ambassador now enters the arc of his assignment which so plainly marks off twentieth-century diplomacy from that of prior times. He begins to make public talks, both formal and informal. He occasionally holds press conferences. All these are designed to clarify his country's policies and attitudes, to explain things that appear in newspapers and other periodicals concerning his country, to bring to earth those unguided missiles of irresponsible comment which start out from his own country from time to time, all thereby to win understanding and friendship for his country. To do this effectively, he must not only be well-informed on his own country and have become aware of the sensibilities of the people whom he is addressing, to avoid malapropisms, but he must be a public speaker of some ability and experience. This is obviously not one of the diplomatist's easier functions, but it is one which the twentieth century has come more and more to require and to emphasize.

In this effort, the diplomatist is assisted by private organizations. In Great Britain, for example, it is customary that the American Ambassador's first public address be made at a dinner given by The Pilgrims. This society was organized by private citizens on both sides of the ocean for the express purpose of contributing to good relations between the United States and Great Britain. It therefore offers an American Ambassador a ready and useful means for getting his speech-making underway. Furthermore, at such a dinner all the members of the British Cabinet are likely to be present, as well as proprietors of the British newspapers and a cross section of British society. This fortunate convenience, however, does not exist everywhere.

Most people utilize language under relatively simple circumstances. They address people they know, in a common language, in a context of similar if not identical cultures, and on matters fairly readily comprehensible to the speaker and the addressed. This is not the case when addressing an audience abroad.

Even when one employs his own language in a foreign country, it ceases to be, in fact, the same medium as at home. It becomes a foreign tongue—one whose words and phrases are uttered to a different people, with a different history, a different culture. This difference in context can lead to different inferences being drawn from those which would be drawn at home. The diplomatist's own language thus harbors considerable risk of misunderstanding. One who deals with international relations witnesses embarrassing situations created by nothing more than a harmless remark which fails to register itself in the intended sense. If this happens too often, a diplomatist's value to his country, of course, begins very rapidly to decline. Hence, even in the use of his own language, the diplomatist must be alertly cognizant of the possibilities of misinterpretation and misunderstanding, and minimize this risk by approaching the same point from a variety of angles. In this way, he can assure a cluster of shots to form unmistakably around the point he is endeavoring to make.

When a diplomatist utilizes a language other than his own, his difficulties multiply. One must know a foreign language extremely well to be at home with it. While a number of diplomatists are competent to read prepared speeches in a foreign tongue, relatively few consider themselves equipped to face an audience and extemporize, unless the tongue be one of the principal languages of the world. Not only is the language different, requiring knowledge of shades of meaning which relatively few people recognize even in their own language, but a certain intuitive sense must be constantly playing in the choice of words. That sense comes only from a fairly intimate familiarity with a people and their culture, as well as with their tongue.

When one must speak through an interpreter, difficulties can still further multiply. Early in my Foreign Service career I was involved in just such a situation and as it was a somewhat critical one I was frankly aghast at the difficulties which suddenly loomed ahead of me. It was necessary on this occasion that I work rapidly and obtain results promptly. This involved prolonged negotiations with people I had never known before and whose country I had never so much as visited. It necessitated also rapid travel, observation and analysis of conditions and opinions in extensive areas of the country, then in some disorder, together with explanations of the objectives of our negotiations to audiences unacquainted with my language. All this, I realized with a sinking heart, had to be done through the mental prism of an interpreter. I was appalled by the refraction which promised to occur as my explanation passed through another mind and another language and returned to me through the same media.

To make certain that my interpreter understood what I said, I resorted to expressing the same idea in several ways. This also reduced the risk that those to whom I was talking might not understand. Naturally, this was a test of ingenuity of expression. To my relief I found one can adapt himself rapidly to this strange and formidable procedure. But I do not recommend it for experimentation in a critical situation.

Before our democratic age, a diplomatist's ability in public speaking made little difference. He was not required to engage in this means of oral presentation. Being obliged only to address himself conversationally to monarchs, ministers and private citizens of influence, he found his ability in oral communication tested solely as a conversationalist and negotiator. But in an age in which large numbers of voters claim some interest in international affairs, a diplomatist must himself have some claim to effective public presentation. He is his government's principal spokesman in the country to which he is assigned: he must be equipped to penetrate all defenses of ignorance and prejudice.

Obviously, this function is not easy to perform. What makes our own country tick is not so easy to explain. Along with a growing complexity of our society and the pressures and influences which operate within it has come a specialization of study and understanding which make shallowness of judgment a pitfall more likely—and more dangerous—than ever.

The diplomatist's public speaking is not limited to people in the country to which he is assigned. We ourselves have resumed, somewhat tentatively, the ancient practice of Greek city states in requiring a certain amount of public accounting by our diplomatists. The Secretary of State and his staff carry the burden of this, but we have been experimenting for some time with diplomatists contributing as well.

This public accounting by the diplomatist occurs along two general lines: discussions with Congressmen and public speeches. The accounting to Congressmen is formally through the system of committee hearings and informally at the diplomatist's mission, when visited by Congressmen seeking clarification of our foreign policies and overseas administration.

Our Congress, just as a popular assembly of ancient Greece,

demands to know the facts of international life and foreign policy; and among the techniques it applies to this end is the committee hearing. Our diplomatists are being brought into this process. They are sometimes called from their distant missions for the purpose of supporting a Departmental request of Congress or clarifying some question of foreign policy or conditions abroad which has been raised in the Congress and which a person with first-hand knowledge can most understandingly handle.

The usual American diplomatist, however, is still more likely to meet Congressmen at his mission than in the United States. Members of Congress now travel much and widely—at least some of them do—and in their annual rounds in search of the facts are not deterred by the elements. This appears to be unique among the parliamentarians of the world, there being no precedent for it and little imitation of it currently by the parliamentarians of other countries, so far as I am aware. But, for the American diplomatist, it is definitely in his book to meet with Congressmen and to explain conditions and policies to them.

The diplomatist is also beginning to appear on the radio at home and to become involved in press conferences when he returns to render accounting. These multiplying functions emphasize the increasing role of speech in the expanding arc of diplomatic performance in the twentieth century.

I believe this has been a healthy development. I know there are those who disagree and feel diplomacy can strike no truce with democracy. However, it is my belief that while diplomacy, in having to explain itself and defend itself on the hustings, may have a pretty rough time of it and lose some of its fineness and sacrifice some of its opportunities for success, it gains from this public accounting a certain wholesomeness in orientation toward the general interest. True enough, the clatter and chatter of a democratic age puts a severe strain upon diplomacy and often scourges it to forensic extravagance, but adjustments are going on at the same time to preserve the efficacy of the process even under these trying conditions.

In any consideration of speech and its role in diplomacy let us not forget that back of it—as back of all things in life—stands character. The ability to speak is but a gift of "sounding brass or a tinkling cymbal" if it be not with character. The reverse is just as true, also. A man with character can overcome the handicaps of speech inadequacies. All of us have at one time or another felt the presence of such a person. Though he speak not a word, his influence is felt. But how much more effective is a man of character if he can speak well!

Chapter 5

MODERN DIPLOMACY AND SPEECH AS A FIELD OF STUDY

S. M. Vinocour

F. S. C. Northrop's very first sentence in his recent book, *The Taming of the Nations,* presents the postulate: "If open diplomacy openly arrived at is to succeed, the people, *without whom the statesmen cannot be effective,* must be informed." The modern diplomat, generally having shed his frock coat of formality and having renounced the secret conference and covenant, is compelled to elicit popular support; and in order to do so, he must energetically seek to inform and convince the people with every method and means at his disposal. Successful modern diplomacy no longer consists solely of governments speaking to governments; today it requires that "ambassadors . . . must talk directly to the people."

This new style of diplomacy has evolved gradually during recent years from the secret diplomacy characteristic of the 17th, 18th, 19th, and early 20th centuries. The classical achievement of the "old" diplomacy was the Congress of Vienna, 1814-15, when the rulers of the then great powers met and settled every disputed question within six months. However, secret diplomacy was dependent upon and responsible to a system of absolute rulers; while the British diplomats were responsible to Parliament, and they did their best to keep Parliament uninvolved until everything was settled. Yet it long had been held in many circles in England that secret diplomacy was "wicked in itself," and this belief became gradually popular. Today every democratic power has to conduct its foreign policy on a moral basis in order to satisfy public opinion. The "new" diplomacy therefore claims to be "public diplomacy"; so far as possible it aims at ". . . actually conducting its business in public." The United States, in particular, ever since Woodrow Wilson's advocacy of "open covenants openly arrived at" in 1919 has encouraged the adoption of and has led in the use of the "open" style in the conduct of international relations. So accepted had this style become that when Franklin Roosevelt reverted to the methodology of secret diplomacy at Teheran and Yalta, his actions aroused considerable criticism.

Yet there is a growing feeling that the new diplomacy has its serious short-comings, too. The increasing international tensions, the Korean war, and the intensification of the "cold war" have led the world to the dangerous precipice of another world war, and the diplomacy seems unable to stem the tide of disastrous events. Walter Lippmann castigates the new diplomacy as the "hoop-la system," by which ". . . every difficult issue, not infrequently a comparatively easy issue, is likely to become insoluble as each actor-statesman rises to such peaks of public righteousness that in public he cannot possibly descend again into common sense." Dr. Grayson Kirk has charged that the sensational demand for publicity in almost every stage of policy making has helped to hamstring the United Nations. "Decorum in international relations is as obligatory as decorum in church," one writer has insisted. Another writer wonders, "Are these recurrent oral fisticuffs in the cold war bound to build up to a violent climax?" Lewis W. Douglas, former American Ambassador to Great Britain, referring to the ". . . advantages of the old diplomacy as a means of settling differences and disputes . . ." between nations, has suggested "that we can do worse than revive some of the lost art of diplomacy." Those who have been disappointed by modern diplomacy have somewhat wistfully and nostalgically called for "A reversal to secret diplomacy," even urging that we ". . . turn off the lights, shut down the microphones, take away the stage props, wash off the makeup, disperse the crowds, and let a few men absent themselves from publicity awhile."

Of course, it is patently impossible to turn back the clock to the days of Metternich, Disraeli, Cavour, *et al.* Such a reversion to the old, secret diplomacy would require the scrapping of the United Nations (since it is a public deliberative body) , the relinquishment of the democratic, popular forms of government (since secret diplomacy thrives best under the system of autocratic rulers) , and the abandonment of all of the modern mass media of communication. In respect to the last mentioned basis of modern diplomacy, the fact must be heavily underscored that the mass media of communication are accessible to the average man in a degree incomprehensible even a half century ago. The world today is equipped with means of communication which, for sheer profusion, variety, speed, vividness, and adaptability, stagger the imagination. These mass media of communication are being used so extensively today in the conduct of international relations that they must be considered an integral and essential part of modern diplomacy. Rather than futilely trying to ignore or curtail them, today's diplomat and his audience would do well to attempt to achieve a better understanding and usage of these media.

Because of the characteristics and requirements of modern diplomacy, the important governmental representatives in world affairs have become in particular, "international spokesmen." Radio, television, the press conference, and the use of important occasions and convocations for important policy statements—all make it abundantly clear that speech has become an important and vital part of the new diplomacy. As Robert T. Oliver has pointed out: "Now the world is engaged in a clumsy but hasty readjustment from fighting one war to preparing for another. In this readjustment, words are prime movers. When the war may come, the basis upon which it will be fought, and formulation of the factors that will probably determine its outcome are all in a basic sense *problems of speech* and by top policy makers are actually considered as such."

Instead of believing that we are retreating nostalgically into the era of secretive foreign policy formulation and execution, a growing number of students are devoting themselves to the study of speech as a medium of international relations;* they are doing so in order to assess realistically the advantages and shortcomings of

---

*The Department of State's Foreign Service Institute now conducts a program of "Functional Training and Language-and-Area Training for the Public Affairs Specialist." Three months of intensive language-training at the Institute is combined with one semester of ". . . carefully integrated area courses in public opinion and international political communication at a university. . . ." (*Prospectus,* Foreign Service Institute, March 23, 1951) Heavy emphasis in the Institute is placed upon "Linguistics," "Metalinguistics," "Microlinguistics," "Cultural Anthropology," "Social Psychology," "Political Science," and upon general course work leading to a broad knowledge ". . . of the themes and media that have been employed and are being employed in the information, education and propaganda programs . . ." of other countries.

speech as the core of modern diplomacy, to attempt to achieve a better understanding of it, and thereby ultimately to attempt the solution of the horde of problems let loose by the new diplomacy in operation.

Lazarsfeld and Merton have pointed out the significance and potential power of the mass media of communication and have suggested that they have a "narcotizing dysfunction," *i.e.,* that they blunt evaluative powers and dull the senses unless properly understood and controlled. Margaret Mead has emphasized the importance of "cross-national communication" in relieving the tensions existing between two countries, and she has suggested that any speaker involved in an international speaking situation apply such principles as "exploration of a friction point," "proper phrasing and translation," and "rapport." Oliver has declared that the speech of diplomacy should be considered as a special and vital area for research—arguing that particular attention must be paid to the problems of obtaining a clearer understanding of how speech influence affects international relations, of gaining better insight and skill in the analysis of the problems of the international spokesman, and of seeking to improve international relations (or more importantly, America's position in world affairs) by improving the techniques and functioning of the modern diplomats.

Believing that "a profession devoted to solving problems in speech should not avoid the challenge to help" our diplomats in the performance of their difficult tasks, Oliver has pioneered in the broad area of international speech by calling for graduate study and increased research in this field. In the fall of 1950 he conducted the first graduate seminar ever devoted to the special study of these problems. The leader and members of this seminar conjointly and tentatively evolved 35 basic postulates concerning international speech; they represent the first tentative analysis and description of, and the preliminary conclusions in the new field of study. The first half of the list of these statements is concerned with the effects of the mass media of communication. Relative to the effect upon *individuals,* it was concluded that:

1. There is a greater interest in world wide affairs.

2. There is a weakening of critical appraisal, increase of conformity.
3. There is a difficulty in distinguishing between truth and untruth.
4. Specific individuals who gain control of mass media have enormously enhanced power.
5. Confused thinking results from conflicts between cultural and ethical standards acquired from national culture and newly perceived standards from other cultures.
   a. Among some groups "tolerance" develops to the extent that ethical and political standards disintegrate.
   b. Among other groups simple stereotypes are eagerly welcomed as an escape from perplexity.
6. There is an increasing tendency to depend on leadership presumed capable of understanding and dealing with the complex world revealed through the mass media.

The effect of the mass media of communication upon *national groups* was summarized as follows:
1. There is a tendency for stronger and more definite polarization of national groups; the in-group becomes more important as the out-groups are better known.
2. The intensive cultivation of domestic public opinion is indispensable to the development of any national policy.
3. Time required for mobilization of public opinion has decreased.
4. Greater knowledge and control of domestic masters of mass media is required by Government in order to know and influence developing public opinion upon international issues.
5. National policies may be immediately and sensitively reshaped in accordance with information immediately received from all parts of the world.
6. Public opinion of the home nation, of friendly, neutral, and enemy nations must be taken into closest account in formulation of foreign policy.

The last six postulates dealing with the effect of modern communications are concerned with *international relations:*
1. A world community becomes hypothetically possible as a result of mass media of communication.

2. Psychological warfare has become possible through mass media.

3. Appeals are made to peoples "over the heads" of their leaders, utilizing such terms as "Wall Street imperialists," "Politburo," "Men in the Kremlin," "ruling classes," etc.

4. Trans-nationalism has become a reality.

5. Diplomatic conferences become a sparring match for public favor.

6. World public opinion becomes a check on national actions.

The next dozen postulates highlight the new and different context in which international speech must be considered by emphasizing the unique effects of an international audience upon world spokesmen:

A. Ambiguity becomes a necessity when speaking to audiences in all parts of the world, having differing standards, differing goals, and differing convictions about the issues discussed.

B. Proposed programs must be phrased in terms having the widest possible acceptance to friendly, neutral, and hostile groups.

C. Verbalisms and stereotypes flourish.

D. "Escape clauses" must be inserted in all policy statements in order that any changes which become necessary may be represented as consistent with the original declaration.

E. National pride must be placated while appealing above and beyond it to a sense of world community.

F. Speakers must possess a depth and sharpness of understanding of the political and cultural factors in every significant portion of the world in order to attain maximum effectiveness.

G. Having an international audience heightens the illusion that talking about a problem is the equivalent of taking action about it; as a contrary tendency, hearing so much talk across national boundary lines cheapens the value of discussion and makes people impatient for direct and immediate action.

H. Spokesmen for nations become defensive-minded as they are aware of appeals directed by hostile nations to their own people; debate sharpens differences and leads to piling up of justifications.

I. As differences become sharper between nations, spokesmen for each nation must become more bellicose in order to avoid domestic charges of appeasement and weakness.

J. Semantic problems (confusion of meaning) are greatly accentuated as audiences expand across national boundary lines.

K. Attempts to interfere with international discussion (by "iron curtains") become major causes of suspicion and resentment.

L. Ideas tend to become attenuated and simplified, reduced to basic concepts with little opportunity for differentiation.

The final five postulates describe the major characteristics of international speech:

A. Puppet speakers talk to shadow audiences.

B. Conciliation and vituperation both become instruments of national policy.

C. Speeches may be fruitfully analyzed for their specificity of appeal to domestic, friendly, neutral, and hostile audiences.

D. "Translatability" of key terms into various languages becomes of prime importance.

E. Carefully defined specific responses must be sought within the overall pattern of the desired total response.

The above postulates, unproved though they may be at the moment, suggest that a different approach to this area of rhetorical criticism may be feasible. Since a modern speech of international consequence given by an international spokesman to a multi-national audience has to deal with markedly different problems than an intra-national speech by a domestic speaker, it is probable that the utilization of traditional rhetorical canons would be inadequate and/or unsatisfactory for description, analysis, and evaluation of speeches of the modern diplomacy, which ". . . has been converted largely into a struggle for dominance over the minds of men."

Chapter 6

STYLE OF SPEECH IN INTERNATIONAL DISCUSSION

IF THE PURPOSE of diplomacy is to settle disputes without war, the world's diplomats would seem to be in need of better training for their jobs. In all history there is no fifty-year span that can match the past half-century in the vast destructiveness of its wars, in the numbers of nations and peoples involved, in the numbers of casualties, in the global effects of even minor conflicts, and in the lack of advantage for the major contending nations. Between World Wars I and II, there were major wars fought between Japan and China (twice), Japan and Russia, the two factions of the Spanish Civil War, and the string of conquests by Fascist Italy and Nazi Germany—besides the civil wars in Mexico and Nicaragua, the drawnout struggle between Bolivia and Peru, and the customary revolutions in other parts of Latin America.

Following the Unconditional Surrender of Italy, Germany, and Japan at the end of World War II, there has been no single interval of peace. Notable among the conflicts were the Dutch-Indonesian War, the Chinese Civil War, the British struggle with the Malayan Communists, the Greek Guerrilla War, the extremely bloody slaughter of Hindu and Muslim populations in India and Pakistan, the French war with Vietminh in Indochina, the successive Arab-Israeli conflicts, the Korean War, the Guatemalan, Argentinian, and Cuban revolutions, the French-Algerian War, the Israel-Egypt Sinai campaign, the British-French invasion of Egypt, the United Kingdom struggle with Muscat and Oman, the Russian suppression of the Hungarian Revolution, the war between Lebanon and Jordan, the prolonged battle over Quemoy and Matsu, the Red Chinese invasion of northern India, the Congolese imbroglio, the conflicts in Laos and Vietnam, the Portuguese war against the Angolese, and the bifurcation of Berlin. The list is not complete and is continually expanding. Obviously, diplomacy in the eras of the League of Nations and the United Nations has not succeeded in curbing the historic record of human warfare.

Obviously, too, there is an urgent need for better diplomacy. No one can doubt that the traditional approaches to diplomacy have proved to be inadequate, nor can we claim that the new international forums have succeeded (though many do feel they may merit the credit of having held at bay the ultimate catastrophe of atomic destruction) .

Besides the impressive record of "hot" wars, this same half-century has been unhappily distinguished by the emergence of the new phenomenon of continuous and total "cold" warfare. A new vocabulary has emerged in which peace means war, democracy means totalitarianism, conquest means liberation, civil liberty means subversion and infiltration, and negotiation means deception. In the Soviet Encyclopedia (1949 edition) Aggression is defined as "the basic method of the foreign policy of imperialist states in the epoch . . . when contradictions in the capitalist world are sharpened to the extreme." Co-existence, according to *Pravda,* November 2, 1953, is struggle between "the historically-doomed forces of reaction and imperialism and the forces of democracy and progress to which the future belongs." According to the *Dictionary of the Russian Language,* Cosmopolitanism is a "reactionary, anti-patriotic, bourgeois outlook on things, hypocritically regarding the whole world as one's fatherland." A Spy was defined over the Sofia Radio in December, 1950, as "Anyone who on any issue and in any guize whatever expresses hostility towards or doubts the correctness of the policy of the Soviet Union." According to the *Short Philosophical Dictionary,* published in Moscow in 1941, Morality "is only that which facilitates the destruction of the old world and strengthens the new, Communist, regime." A Patriot, as defined in Harry Hodginson's *The Language of Communism* (1954) , "is anyone who believes that the interests of his own country necessarily and always coincide with those of the USSR." A Revolutionary is defined by Stalin, in his *Collected Works,* 1949, Volume X, as "he who without argument, unconditionally, openly and honestly without secret military consultations is ready to protect and defend the USSR." The new vocabulary indicates clearly the nature of the new technique of cold war: the bewitchment of intelligence through the misuse of language. Stalin was highly praised in his lifetime, by his followers, as an astute student of language, who "revealed the role played by language as an instrument for the development of society," and who pictured the communicator as an "engineer of human souls." In the Communist arsenal of psychological warfare, words ceased to be symbols for reality and became symbols of intent. Their intention of ignoring or distorting reality, however, runs so far counter to ordinary human expectation that only the sophisticated and the alert are able to protect their minds from the planned bewitchment. Meanwhile, diplomats representing the democracies have had to work out some special language techniques of their own to meet the conditions of the cold war.

The new need demands a new emphasis in the selection and in the training of diplomats. Traditionally, education for foreign service consisted largely of study of history, political science, economics, and languages. Today this has to be supplemented with work in anthropology, linguistic theory, propaganda analysis, public speaking, discussion, and conference.

Special consideration, indeed, is required to insure the development of consummate skill in the various forms of speech. Diplomats today talk less in closed sessions to one another than they do in open meetings, where, indirectly, they are addressing international audiences, friendly, neutral, and hostile, all over the world. Even when they speak directly to one another, the audiences they really have in mind are the selected groups of opinion-formers in the hundred-odd nations. Diplomacy no longer is merely government speaking to government; it is government appealing over the heads of government to the peoples behind the leaders.

President Harry Truman took explicit note of this change of direction, on March 2, 1952, in his internationally broadcast speech dedicating *Courier,* the new "Voice of America" radio ship. "There is a terrific struggle going on," he pointed out, "to win the minds of people throughout the world." He went on, "Your government may try to make you believe . . ., but I want you to know . . ." The deliberate effort to create disaffection and distrust among peoples toward their own governments had officially become a policy of the democracies, as it long had been for the Communists.

When diplomats confront one another across conference tables, they are acutely aware that they, all of them, are but *puppet speakers addressing shadow audiences.* The diplomat does not and can not speak for himself; he can only phrase ideas that are determined for him back home, by those who make the national policies. And regardless of how persuasive his arguments may be, the actual listeners seated around the table are powerless to follow their own judgment as to how his message should be evaluated. When a point of decision approaches, the meeting has to be adjourned while the negotiators await "instructions" on how to respond, cabled from their home governments. Actual negotiation, in the traditional sense, has been rendered impossible by publicity (which makes it a gladatorial combat before the public) and by our rapid means of communication (which separates the decision-making from the discussion) .

It is partly for these reasons that "summit meetings" of Heads of State have become a necessity. In these, to some extent, the power to make and alter policy is actually represented within a private conference scene. The extent of this power of immediate negotiation, however, is less than it appears, even when the Chief Executives of the Great Powers meet face to face. For any decision requiring a change of established policy, the concurrence of the legislative branches is needed, and time must be allowed for a gradual re-education of public opinion. Both in dictatorships and in democracies, the leaders are, in varying degrees, but spokesmen for those whom they represent. This is a prime reason why summit meetings are extremely rare and why care is taken beforehand to insist that no specific issues will be discussed and no concrete decisions will be reached. One major effect of the development of mass communication has been to delay and to diffuse (some would say to dissipate) the power of formulating policies.

Out of these various considerations, a new style of speaking in international conferences has become necessary. We shall now examine the principal elements of this new international speech.

IMPERSONALITY

Diplomats, as we have noted, are spokesmen, not speakers; agents, not principals. The voice may be the voice of Gromyko or of Adlai Stevenson, but the words are those of the Kremlin or the

White House. What governmental representatives say has only an incidental relationship to their own convictions. Neither does the form of their speech necessarily reflect their own personalities. Typically, they are mouthpieces, somewhat like the loudspeaker of a public address system. They say what they are instructed to say, and their manner indicates joviality, irritability, firmness, or flexibility, whatever their policy-makers may indicate.

Likewise, the governmental representatives to whom they speak must respond strictly in accordance with their instructions. The concepts of *ethos* (or the persuasive attributes of personality) and of circularity of response between speaker and listeners—which are extremely important in ordinary speaking—may be applied only with great caution and qualification to the needs of modern diplomacy. As we trace the history of some fifteen years of negotiations on atomic disarmament, for example, we find that the representatives on both sides have frequently changed, but the arguments remain the same. We find, too, that when a break-down appears imminent, the hostile sentiments expressed may be converted to an appearance of sweet reasonableness. Thus the talks are kept alive, even though all the participants realize that they are no more than window-dressing, maintaining a semblance of negotiation while the real determination of policy is being studied in the several national capitals. The men who bear the labels of "negotiators" are like characters in a play, reading the lines that are written for them, and playing the parts to which they are assigned. What their personal opinions may be is a matter of very little or absolutely no consequence.

At the United Nations and in periodically-staged high-level conferences held by foreign ministers, impersonality equally prevails, but with a difference. Men such as Litvinov and Briand, in the period between the two world wars, and such men as Vishinsky, Molotov, Acheson, and Dulles, in more recent times, did indeed have personality types that were of great symbolic significance. Litvinov represented a genuine belief in peace to be achieved through mutual forebearance, just as Molotov represented a conviction that the national purposes of Russia can best be secured through intimidation. Dean Acheson was known for his lofty appeals to common interest and John Foster Dulles for his righteous moral indignation. Each nation, meanwhile, had also other spokesmen of other characteristics: Gromyko with his mask of urbane impenetrability, Warren Austin with his crusading spirit and Philip Jessup who was noted for his power of coldly logical analysis. These varied spokesmen are alternated as their governments seek to create one or another impression. Newspaper readers may come to think of one man as an "appeaser," and another as a "war monger." But the diplomats themselves are fully aware that each is merely fulfilling a function required by his Government.

Nikita Khrushchev represents still another way in which impersonality becomes an instrument of diplomacy and propaganda. The exuberance, expressiveness, and mad-cap exhibitionism of his personality have become hallmarks of the international scene. But only the naive still think of him (as many did after his first emergence into leadership of the USSR) as a man ruled by his emotions. Quite the contrary is true; no other character on the world stage is so shrewdly aware of the value of playing many parts to develop differing aspects of policy. In the classic experiment performed by Ivan Petrovich Pavlov, the great Russian psychologist, dogs and other animals were subjected to nervous break-downs by random and meaningless alternations of pleasant and painful stimuli. It was found that animals could make satisfactory adjustments to any systematic pattern of behavior, no matter how much it lacked of justice or common sense. If their good behavior was punished and their bad behavior rewarded, they would be confused for a time but would soon adapt to this strange system. However, when utter unpredictability of the relations between behavior and response was introduced, they soon displayed signs of emotional disintegration. Khrushchev has become a prime artist in the application to diplomacy of this Pavlovian discovery. "What will the man do next?" has become a puzzle that makes relatively unimportant the question of what his real personality may be. Instead of alternating his spokesmen to express divergent strains of the zig-zag Communist policies, Mr. K himself enacts the entire orchestra. What he may be like today carries no discernible hint of what he may be like tomorrow.

To try to judge the trends of diplomacy in terms of particular personalities is a hopeless task. For diplomacy is essentially depersonalized.

FACTS VERSUS POLICIES

Only the uninitiated expect diplomatic speech to accord strictly with objective reality. Some governments are more prone than others to distort or misrepresent facts. Western diplomats have long ago learned that the Communists regard deception in diplomacy as comparable to camouflage in war. At the Second World Congress of the Communist International, held at Moscow in 1920, one of the directives adopted was that "Each Communist representative must remember that he is not a 'legislator' who is bound to seek agreements with other legislators but an agitator of the party, detailed into the enemy's camp in order to carry out the orders of the party there." Allied diplomats at international conferences have learned that their Communist opposite-numbers have remarkable facility in lying even when they know that the other diplomats know that what they are saying is a deliberate lie. They consider this as being in the same category as having Marines in the jungle wear clothing splotched with green and brown, to make it resemble the foliage. Deception is useful if it succeeds and praiseworthy in intent even if it should be discerned. This the diplomats know, though the public sometimes is confused and may believe that a straightforward avowal must have at least some dependability.

The Communists, however, are not alone in this practice. Even the most honorable governments reserve the right to select and "interpret" the facts which they consider relevant, or helpful, in dealing with any issue. When a crisis or issue is to be confronted, the preliminary stage is an intra-governmental policy to formulate the correct "policy line" toward the situation. Considerable efforts are made to determine what the correct facts may be, but the final decision reached is based not alone on the facts but also on national necessity or convenience. The "policy line' concerning what government spokesmen will say publicly about, say, the Yalta Conference, is shaped in terms of what will be helpful, rather than necessarily what is true. Negotiators, in Ralph Waldo Emerson's phrase, are "retained attorneys," pledged to achieve stated aims, not social scientists dedicated to the depiction of reality. Hence it is that the public, even in the democracies, is warned repeatedly by its leaders not to judge too strictly what is being done or said, on the grounds that only the "inner circle" really know what the facts are.

Considerable confusion in the public mind concerning international affairs could be avoided if only this one characteristic of diplomatic speech were fully understood: that facts are facts, and policy-lines are policy-lines, and seldom do the two categories precisely converge. Sometimes they are widely divergent. For example, following the signing of the truce in Korea, in 1953, it was commonplace for high-level American officials to say to one another in private that the war could and should have been won, while publicly affirming the policy-line that a principal achievement of the Administration was the ending of the Korean War.

TECHNICAL VOCABULARY

Commentators frequently object to the apparently stilted and unreal language used by diplomats. When a diplomat says, "Under the circumstances that subsist, and considering the positions stated, and reserving the right for further exposition of related questions, but without implying a precedent in regard to contiguous considerations, the answer is in the negative," laymen well may wonder why a simple "No!" would not be better. One of the functions of diplomacy is to keep open all possible channels for additional adjustments of stated positions. This function has led to the development of a vocabulary of diplomacy specifically designed to minimize disagreements, or to soften their effects, thereby encouraging further exploration of common ground.

For this purpose, *sanctions* has been adopted to replace *force*. A diplomat may "take a grave view of a situation," or indicate that "The consequences will be inevitably influential in affecting the stage of retaliatory reaction." But only when every other recourse has failed will he say bluntly, "In such a case we will go to war." Hair-line distinctions are made, as in the United Nations offer to accept oral assurances from the Communists, rather than requiring a written pledge, not to build airfields in northern Korea during the truce negotiations at Panmunjom. To protect national pride and prestige, policies are *adjusted* rather than *reversed*. Military armament is subdivided into *aggressive* and *defensive* weapons —the latter often being those on which control agreements cannot be reached. Boundary lines are *rectified*; treaties are *revised;* pledges are *reconsidered* or *negated by events* or *interpreted*. Without such jargon, negotiation would be even more difficult than it is at present.

Sometimes the purpose of this technical vocabulary is to veil meanings that are unpalatable; at other times its purpose is to achieve precision and exactitude of discriminatory statement. Such phrases as "brinkmanship," "agonizing re-appraisal," and "massive retaliation" are good for headlines but difficult to interpret. When the occasion demands it, diplomats must be skilled in saying precisely what is meant, no more and no less. Hugh R. Wilson, in his autobiography, *The Education of a Diplomat* (1938), gave central importance to this ability: "A wide lack in my earlier education was laid bare to me in a few weeks. I have been approximating. No one had ever driven me to exactitude of statement. There grew gradually in my mind a love of accuracy and conciseness, a hatred of vagueness and circumlocution."

The harm that may be done when a public figure of consequence speaks on international affairs without using the technical vocabulary of diplomacy may be illustrated by turning back to an earlier time, when Senator Shelby M. Cullon, in 1895, orated:

> It is time that someone woke up and realized the necessity of annexing some property. We want all this northern hemisphere, and when we begin to reach out to secure these advantages we will begin to have a nation and our lawmakers will rise above the grade of politicians and become true statesmen.

Nevertheless, precision of statement is valuable only when precise positions need to be defined. Often avoidance of an issue is better than meeting it head on. Then a different type of diplomatic speech is required.

INTENTIONAL AMBIGUITY

Often during international conferences, Allied negotiators complain that they can not understand what the Communist delegation is presenting. Similarly, in the earlier stages of any negotiation, it is commonplace for all the delegations deliberately to state their own proposals and their replies to what is presented with calculated vagueness. The intent is to require the opposition to restate what has been said, as they understand it, or to induce spokesmen to present their positions in a variety of ways, in the hope that by inadvertence some unintended meaning may be revealed. To the public this may appear to be sheer incompetence, but it is playing the fool with wisdom. Both sides remain alert to seize upon whatever formulation of meaning most nearly correlates with their own policies. The public demand that diplomacy should become more "plain and straight-forward" ignores the value of ambiguity in preserving a useful middle ground of unresolved opinion.

Ambiguity has another value in incomplete and developing situations. This is to facilitate changes in policy to accord with whatever opportunities may arise or to retreat when necessary without seeming to do so. One of the charges often made against Soviet diplomacy, and sometimes against that of the United States, it that it is too "inflexible" to permit needed changes. The English have long prided themselves upon their ability to maintain an appearance of clumsy uncertainty while watching and waiting for a chance to attain a desired objective. One of their chief criticisms of American diplomacy has been our greater tendency to clarify and define our intentions. On the issue of the independence of western Berlin and the right of access by Allied nations to that city, we have had no intention of permitting any ambiguity; for to do so would simply erode the agreement we have sought to maintain. The Communists, on the other hand, have sought for years to introduce ambiguity and uncertainty, with the aim of making our position less stable.

For forty centuries China maintained its position as the "Middle Kingdom" (not the "dominant power") in North Asia by skillful use of *wu-wei,* or ambiguity. Refusing to define China's relations to surrounding nations, avoiding demands on them, yet persistently reiterating its role as "Big Brother" to the other states, Chinese statesmen wove a net of inter-relationships which bound a dozen nations into an undefined Chinese confederacy. Even in our own time, this confusion of sovereignty has remained unclarified, making it possible for the Chinese to claim or renounce claims on Inner and Outer Mongolia, Manchuria, Korea, Tibet, and areas of Burma and India, as suited their convenience. The nature of the British Commonwealth for many years remained almost equally ambiguous—and is still happily amenable to differing interpretations to fit differing circumstances. In trying to maintain peace among nations that are above all laws by virtue of being sovereign, diplomacy must transmute "Say what you mean" into "Say something that can be interpreted to mean whatever may prove to be convenient in circumstances that cannot be foreseen."

UNINTENTIONAL AMBIGUITY

Language differences sometimes introduce into international conferences ambiguities that are not intended. Since French was abandoned as the customary language of diplomacy, expert translators have become indispensable. The United Nations in its early years engaged sixty-five interpreters, then seventy-two, and, now that its membership has virtually doubled, the problems of translation have multiplied. Not only the differences in languages but the difference in speakers has proved troublesome. The fact that Vishinsky habitually spoke at the extremely rapid rate of 300 words a minute imposed especially heavy demands upon his interpreter. Able as the translators are, the diplomats seated about the conference rooms often feel left out of immediate communication with their opposite numbers. This is especially true when speakers use folk sayings and idioms to express precise shades of meaning (or to blunt the definitiveness of their remarks). The most experienced interpreters at the United Nations feel their incapacity when they hear, "In my country there is an old saying . . ."

Translation is but an awkward vehicle for transferring the meaning of colloquialisms.

On occasion problems of translation are almost incapable of solution. When the Moscow Conference of 1945 recommended a four-power trusteeship for Korea, the only Korean term that seemed appropriate was *bo ho kook,* which had been used to denominate the Japanese Protectorate of 1905-1910. A new term, *shin tak tong chi,* was devised by Allied strategists; but this did not prove to make international supervision any more palatable to the Korean people. As is well known, even "translation" from English to American speech offers many difficulties. *Compromise,* for example, carries in England the favorable connotation of joining together the best elements in two proposals; but in America it connotes the surrender of good and the acceptance of evil—as is indicated in our saying that a girl's virtue or a man's honor may be compromised. In effect, to Americans compromise means appeasement. In 1951, when Sir Benegal Rau of India offered in the United Nations a *conciliation* of the Korean War, the term connoted in India the successful method of Gandhian passive resistance. To both the Western nations and the Communists, it signified "weakness." Even when the effort of the diplomats is to be unavoidably precise, misunderstandings across linguistic and cultural barriers are often inevitable.

CAUTIOUS PHRASING

The speech of diplomacy is traditionally cautious—avoiding dogmatism, ultimatums, and threats. To call a person "diplomatic" means that he is pleasantly conciliatory in his speech and manners. A fine example of such conciliatory carefulness is provided from an experience of Lincoln's opponent, Senator Stephen A. Douglas, during his trip to France before the Civil War. While he was having an audience with the Emperor Louis Napoleon and Princess Eugenie, "the Empress undertook to rebuke America's anxiety to acquire Cuba. 'Were I Queen of Spain,' she said spiritedly, 'I would spend the last coin and shed the last drop of Spanish blood before the United States should have even a foothold on the island.' The Senator bowed very low and answered: 'Madam, were you the Queen of Spain, it would not be necessary to spend money or shed blood, as love would keep all your subjects loyal.' Eugenie's beautiful face broke into a smile and the retort courteous was the talk of the Court." Thus the occasion is described by George Fort Milton in his book, *The Eve of Conflict: Stephen A. Douglas and the Useless War* (1934).

But it is not wholly accidental that the illustration is more than a hundred years in the past. In our time, diplomatic caution is not always marked by good manners. Quite typical of diplomatic interchanges in our day is the reply made by Vishinsky to Dean Acheson's charge, in 1950, that Russia was uniting the northern Chinese provinces into the Soviet Union: "Acheson stated all these awkwardnesses in order to put a good face on a bad game, to slander the foreign policy of the USSR, and by this token to place the blame on the USSR for the failure of his own policy." The bad manners were deliberately offensive; nevertheless, nothing was said that could in itself precipitate a crisis.

Despite the contemporary renunciation of conciliatory phrasing, diplomats exercise great care to avoid passing the point of no return—unless war has been settled upon as the only acceptable solution. Newspaper readers may get the impression that the Soviet-United States debates in the United Nations signal or indeed induce irreducible differences of policy. Actually, the vitriol conceals from the casual eye the protagonists' careful reservations which indicate their intention of seeking peaceful solutions.

The careful reservations, often ingeniously concealed, are what the diplomats learn to search for. This is why the State Department habitually responds to the receipt of a communication from Russia, for example, with the statement that the document is being studied. Few statements on international relations are drawn without containing an "escape clause" that could later be used to nullify all or part of it. A famous example is the statement in the Cairo Declaration issued by Franklin Roosevelt, Winston Churchill, and Chiang Kai-shek on December 1, 1943, declaring that they were "determined that in due course Korea shall be free and independent." *Due course* could mean anything or nothing. It could mean immediately after Korea's liberation from Japan, or it could mean at any convenient time thereafter. Similarly, at the Summit Conference in Geneva, in July, 1955, Bulganin replied to Eisenhower's demand for re-unification of Germany by saying, "The Soviet Government, now as in the past, favors the unification of Germany in conformity with the national interests of the German people and the security of Europe." The conditions were deliberately rendered sufficiently vague to leave Russia free to take any position events might seem to make desirable.

An interesting commentary on the diplomatic habit of speaking with ambiguity and caution was offered in a 1957 interview Harvey Breit of the New York *Times* held with George Kennan, whose *Russia Leaves the War* had just received the National Book nonfiction award. When Breit asked him why he didn't try his hand at fiction, Kennan replied, "I've been in the foreign service too long to write a novel. One's entire life is devoted to holding back, to *not* divulging things, to, in short, being a diplomat." This, presumably, is what Will Rogers meant when he defined a diplomat as "a guy who says what he don't mean in ways people can't understand." Often the function of diplomatic speech is to avoid being clear.

SUBSTANCE VERSUS FORM

In ordinary human relationships, the desire to "shine" underlays a vast amount of social talk. In an argument, the disputants want to win in a way that will make their superiority evident to the others. Many a time we sacrifice the opportunity to win agreement through conciliation for the greater satisfaction of attaining an ego-triumph over an associate. In diplomacy this is a kind of satisfaction that is far too costly to be afforded. On the contrary, effective diplomacy demands that if one side is to win the substance of a dispute, the other side should be given the outward appearance of victory. When John Steelman was winning a high reputation for his work as the United States Mediator of labor disputes, during the Great Depression, he explained his success by saying, "I give the decision to one side and the words to the other." This is what the diplomats aim to do. Nations have very sensitive pride. Diplomats must remain able to represent to their people back home that their national cause is triumphant. Hence, when an international problem is settled, one of the cardinal results that must be achieved is to "save face" for the nation that comes out second best.

When Franklin Roosevelt was at Casablanca, during World War II, he startled Winston Churchill and astounded the world's diplomats by saying casually in a news conference that the war would end only with the "unconditional surrender" of the Fascist powers. Many have felt that this statement resulted in prolonging the war. The term has meaning militarily, but can only be damaging diplomatically. Japan, Germany, and Italy, all, as a matter of fact, emerged from World War II into greater economic strength and with perhaps sounder political positions than they had before the war. Unconditional Surrender meant little except in terms of humiliation. And for this a high price had to be paid in time, money, and lives.

During the two years of negotiation that were required to end the fighting in Korea, a primary question was where the line of demarcation between the north and the south should be drawn. We had taken a stand for a line that would be defensible militarily —and that would be far enough north to indicate that the United Nations had "defeated" the Communists. The Communists, on the other hand, had demanded a restoration of the 38th parallel division—to demonstrate that nothing of substance had been accomplished by the war. After many months of discussion, the solution finally reached was a line that bulged northward of the 38th parallel in the east and south of it in the west. Both sides could claim victory, (and both have).

SPECIAL PROCEDURES

What we have learned about the conduct of discussion in our ordinary business and civic affairs has little pertinence to international conferences. Diplomatic gatherings have their own special parliamentary rules. Their procedures are drawn primarily to recognize the sovereign independence of all participants and to safeguard complete independence from any majority decision. Some of these may be enumerated as follows:

1. The chairmanship may be held alternately by representatives of two or more participants, taking care that each "side" is given an equal role. When this is not practical, conferences are held with no chairman at all. In these latter cases (represented by the continuing conferences between the two sides in the Korean Truce) the representatives take their places at the table and one delegate or another simply starts talking. When no one has anything else to say, they disband. Of course, when a chairman is presiding, he opens and closes the meeting formally and "recognizes" those who wish to speak. Such chairmanship functions as summarizing various stages of the discussion and even calling for votes are seldom utilized.

2. Far from being "tentative minded" and seeking mutually agreeable joint solutions, the participants take care to emphasize the "unalterable" nature of the policy lines of their governments. Special techniques are sometimes employed to wear down the opposition. Lengthy and repetitive speeches have become a hallmark of Communist delegates. At one meeting of the Panmunjom Truce Conference, General Nam Il, the chief Communist delegate, sat immobile for two hours and eleven minutes, following a question asked by Vice-Admiral C. Turner Joy, the chief U. N. delegate. Neither side said a word, while the long minutes ticked by. Finally, Admiral Joy pushed back his chair, and the delegates all marched stolidly out.

In a meeting of the Korea-Japan Conference, in 1952, the chief Japanese delegate, doubtlessly acting on instructions, began to prod the Korean delegation by irritatingly interjecting frequently into his comments, "Don't you see?" Meanwhile, another Japanese delegate said never a word but seemingly fulfilled his function by responding to every Korean comment with a cynical smile of rejection. On the other hand, the chief of the Korean delegation made frequent use of such phrases as, "We believe in being frank and open," and "We have nothing to conceal," as a means of making a virtue of undiplomatic criticism of past Japanese policies toward Korea. The conference lasted for several months but adjourned (as have several others subsequently) with no results.

3. As another specialized device, "trial balloons," or demands

that might lead to a break-down of negotiations, are commonly offered in tentative fashion by subordinate members of the delegations. Thus, they may be more easily amended or abandoned, without loss of prestige, if they are rejected.

4. Questions which in ordinary parliamentary bodies would be referred to the Committee of the Whole for discussion and solution are commonly referred to sub-committees, where they may be thoroughly explored, but where no decisions can be reached. The purpose is to avoid bringing issues to a head unless or until the home governments have decided whether to agree or to disagree on a solution.

DIPLOMACY AND PUBLICITY

Diplomatic conferences are particularly plagued by the outpouring of publicity during their day-by-day deliberations. When the domestic and world publics are informed concerning every proposal advanced, they become agitated when later modifications are accepted. True negotiation is prevented by cries of "appeasement" and "surrender." Woodrow Wilson's ideal of "open covenants openly arrived at" has proved to be all but impossible to achieve. What it really means is that few agreements of any kind are possible—except such as may be worked out in secret through regular diplomatic channels, before a conference is even held. Diplomats are well aware of the problem. On the other hand, "secret diplomacy" has fallen into such ill repute that such closed meetings as were held at Teheran, Yalta, and Potsdam are probably now impossible except during actual hostilities.

When an international meeting is convened among major nations, often at Geneva—or at the United Nations—more than a thousand newsmen assemble. Regular press briefings are held by major delegations following each day's sessions, where the proceedings are often represented quite differently by the spokesmen for the various nations. Meanwhile, the newsmen labor assiduously to develop "lines of contact" with representatives who will be in the meetings, or with members of their advisory staffs. "Leaks" are commonplace—partly because every delegation is jockeying to win the favor of important newsmen in the hope of geeting better publicity for its own views.

The situation is similar to what would happen if love affairs had to be carried on under spot-lights surrounded by a curious crowd. Little genuine wooing is possible. The conferences are forced to assume the characteristics of gladatorial contests. Yet the public has been educated to take an interest in what is happening; and legislative bodies, as well as citizens, back home are extremely suspicious of efforts to maintain secrecy. No solution seems to be in prospect. The genuine negotiation often has to be conducted very circumlocutionarily at dinner parties or in other social meetings.

THE AGENDA

One of the important considerations in the preparation for any diplomatic conference is the jockeying for advantage in the formulation of the agenda. The relations of nations are extremely complex. Any question that may arise has a long history. In seeking settlements of specific issues, each side desires to claim relevancy for certain sets of facts and to eliminate others as irrelevant. Tremendous advantage (in terms at least of favorable publicity) could be won simply in terms of an agenda favoring one side or the other. If you owe a man money and he wishes to get together to talk about it, you would profit by diverting at least a share of the discussion to the fact that his dog digs holes in your garden. Just so do nations seek to introduce onto the agenda the topics that promise to give them an advantage.

The difficulty and importance of the agenda are illustrated by the fact that in the Spring of 1950 representatives of the Big Powers met for fourteen weeks in Paris, struggling without success to agree on a list of subjects their Foreign Ministers would be willing to discuss. Before the Cease Fire Conference could open in Korea in 1951, six weeks were consumed in debate on what topics would be covered. Even then, in order to get the conference started, the agenda was phrased so ambiguously that for the next two years there was constant wrangling over what subjects were really relevant. In many conferences, the most important work that is done is the drawing of an agenda. Normally nations are unwilling to confer with one another unless or until they have already decided what the outcome is likely to be.

CONCLUSION

Since collective security cannot displace war until a suitable method for conducting diplomacy is developed, one of the major tasks confronting humanity is to devise conference techniques that meet the new demands of the mass media of communication. The problem deserves attention and support similar to that devoted to space satellites and modern weapons. What has happened within the past generation is that the old diplomacy has been rendered impossible and we are still struggling to find new methods adequate to take its place.

Diplomacy has been converted largely into a struggle for the minds of men. Distinctions between diplomacy and propaganda have become to a large degree academic. International conferences have been degraded into sounding boards for propaganda rather than sessions for the solution of problems. The inadequacy of the present methods is well understood. In the immediately preceding pages we have stressed the glare of publicity and its effects upon national pride and prestige. We have also discussed the influence of cultural and linguistic differences. The fact that sovereign nations, by definition, are finally subject to no law except their own concept of their own interests is another vastly complicating factor. Diplomats have incredibly difficult tasks to perform. One solution that might ease the problems would be the elimination of sovereign nations by incorporating them all into a single World Government. This may be the eventual outcome; but diplomats cannot wait upon visionary future possibilities. Meanwhile, perhaps the general public can help a bit if it will understand the problems and exercise a greater degree of forebearance. If we want to "talk" rather than "fight" our way to a settlement of world problems, we must allow our chosen representatives the leeway required by the real discussion process. In view of present circumstances, this, too, may be no more than a visionary hope. Meanwhile, in a later chapter we shall examine the means by which the Communist nations seek to advance their own purposes and to frustrate ours through their own special type of rhetoric.

Chapter 7

THE VARIED RHETORICS OF INTERNATIONAL RELATIONS

W E ARE ALL ISLANDS," wrote George Eliot, the nineteenth century English novelist, "shouting lies to one another across seas of misunderstanding." She was thinking of individuals; her judgment would be even truer if it were applied to communications transmitted from one cultural group to another. A "cultural group" is a vague term that can only be defined arbitrarily. In one sense the Anglo-American and Western European peoples comprise a cultural group, as distinguished from the Asian, the African, the Middle Eastern, and the South American groupings. But when we examine peoples so closely related as those of Great Britain and the United States, we find significant cultural differences that must be bridged. And within the United States, there are genuinely germain differences between such cultural entities as the Negroes, the Jews, the Catholics, and the Protestants—or the farmers, the wage workers, and the professional class. The arbitrary definition we shall use is to define a culture group as a population having a common tradition sufficiently cohesive so that its manners and habits of thinking tend to be similar and, conversely, tend to be different from those of other cultural groups. The looseness of the definition reflects the ambiguity of the data with which we must work. The very vagueness of the problem is a major reason why international communication presents so serious a problem.

Politically, peoples are organized under sovereign governments. For many important considerations—affecting wars, economic barriers, treaties, currencies, and immigration, for examples—the nation is itself the most significant cultural group of our times. Nevertheless, there are also important trans-national influences that must be taken into account. Muslim nations have demonstrated their feeling of commonality as they look out upon the rest of the world, though they also cling sufficiently to their differences to resist uniting into a single nation. Christianity, Confucianism, Taoism, and Buddhism are all trans-national influences of great potency, although they are not strong enough to prevent bitter animosities within each of these cultural settings. The point of this chapter is that major cultures do impose habits of thought and feeling upon their constituent populations and that as we try to communicate across cultural lines we need to employ varied rhetorics.

Anthropologists are accumulating convincing evidence that mankind cannot be divided into mutually exclusive groups called "races." We have all imbibed considerable understanding of the brave proposition of Robert Burns that, regardless of race, religion, or social class, "A man's a man, for a' that." From many points of view it is both possible and eminently desirable to melt away the differences and deal with the basic humanity we all have in common.

Nevertheless, cultural anthropology also makes the very sound point that *nurture* as well as *nature* does make a difference. Many of the characteristics we think of as being "in-born" are really "in-bred." Our characters, our temperament, our personality, our interests, and our abilities are all affected deeply by the society in which we grow up. Much of the "social agglomerate"—the curious and unsystematic mixture of ideals and fears, of ambitions and sympathies—that we take for granted has been taught us by our parents, our schools, our churches, and the huge apparatus of publicity and propaganda that creates and serves what we call public opinion. Despite the political oratory about "One World," every major community has its own customs, its own way of thinking, its own moral codes, its own standards of value. Even our most precious sensibilities and vital urges—such as the determination to "do right" and "avoid wrong"—are products of education. Much more so is this true of the specific actions we classify as "right" or "wrong." And they are learned differently in different societies.

Now, what has this to do with rhetoric? It has a great deal to do with the Aristotelian rhetoric we have traditionally been concerned with, and even more to do with the "new rhetoric" advocated by such men as Ogden, and Richards, and Kenneth Burke, and Benjamin Lee Whorf.

Both the old and the new rhetoric are in some ways precise and in some ways extremely diffuse and inclusive. Both insist that *rhetoric is a mode of thinking,* and especially a mode of influencing the ways in which other people think. The emphasis is upon "finding all available means" of shifting the opinions of those to whom we talk. Aristotle was concerned with what the speaker himself says and does; the new rhetoricians are concerned with the whole pattern of influences that converge upon the communicative act from the totality of the social situation. Both stress the necessity of analyzing the audience and the occasion in order that the speaker may say what needs to be said, in the manner in which it needs to be said, so that he may achieve the effect he desires with his particular hearers. Both the Aristotelian and the "new" rhetorics are so inclusive that we have insisted, with some justification, that they are adequate as guides for any speaker under any and all circumstances.

Nevertheless, it seems to me there are some presumptions underlying the way in which we have commonly studied and taught our traditional rhetoric that *impose* rather than *remove* barriers when we try to use these principles on the international scene.

The rhetoric of Aristotle is, of course, far from being static. Cicero enlarged it in terms of style, Quintilian in terms of ethos, and Whately did some recasting to take account of the equalitarian teachings of John Locke. In our own day the scepticism of Hume and the new scientific empiricism have modified our interpretation of the old logic. Through the discipline of General Semantics we have tried to adjust our methodology to deal with elements of dynamism and instability identified by psychiatrists and the social psychologists. And through the Sapir-Whorf hypothesis concerning linguistic determinism, we have tried to come to grips with the fact that each of the two thousand-odd languages imposes to some degree its own pattern of perception as well as of thought. Surely, there is no need to advocate openmindedness to new influences upon or new interpretations of the meaning of rhetoric. It is true in rhetoric as it is in science these days that "nothing is stable but flux."

Nevertheless, we limit ourselves more than we realize. We

limit our view of how to deal with other peoples simply by the fact
that our own culture is so early and so deeply imbedded into our
individual psyches that we find it honestly very difficult to conceive
of other systems of value, or other modes of thinking. On many
occasions I have observed Americans in Korea who felt that if
those people are too stupid to learn English, they're just stupid.
And I can testify that it is easier to smile at this error than to avoid
it. Strongly as I feel myself a part of the Korean scene, I must admit that many a time, as I have listened to cabinet members
stumblingly trying to express elementary ideas in broken English,
I have had to remind myself that their problem is not intellectual
but linguistic. As a matter of fact, even their linguistic abilities
far surpass my own. But if our attitudes about language give us a
clue to the problem, the problem itself is much more than linguistic.

The rhetoric with which we are concerned, whether Aristotelian or "new," is developed particularly for the Anglo-American
and Western European society. When we think of influencing
people, we think of free men who have the right to cast free ballots;
we think of rational beings, beset by emotionalism, but finally
"available" to persuasion that is factually and logically sound. We
think of propositions that are worthy of discussion because they
are based upon probabilities, concerning which various speakers
may reasonably present various interpretations. And with our
emphasis upon the sovereignty of the people and the doctrine of
the "greatest good for the greatest number," we accept (sometimes
with bad grace) the conclusion finally rendered by majority vote.
It is honestly and fundamentally difficult for us to realize that *no
single one of these presumptions is universal*. This is the major
barrier that stands in the way of an international rhetoric.

If the Speech profession is to make a helpful contribution to
internationalism—if we are to be able to help our diplomats do a
better job in our multiple and ever-increasing dealings with other
peoples around the world—it is my belief that we shall have to stop
using rhetoric in the singular and commence using it in the plural.
I think the facts of life indicate that there is not just one rhetoric—
instead, there are many rhetorics. This is to say, there are many

different modes of thinking, many different standards of value, many different ways in which influence must be exerted if it is to be effective.

Let me illustrate with some brief reference to the Shinto rhetoric of Japan.* So far as I know, no one has tried to systematize the rhetoric of Shintoism. The Japanese themselves seem to understand it in the way we understand the basic values of our own civilization—because it is bred into their habit structure. When they seek to influence one another, they do not address appeals to general or universal motives, for they conceive of the personality not as one whole but as segmentalized into four major parts: the circles of *jin, giri, ko,* and *chu.* It is relatively easy for them to shift behavioral codes from one circle to another without much "psychic cost." We, of course, shift our codes of conduct also: one for church, one for family, one for business, one for dealing with strangers.* But since we think in terms of the integrity of the whole individual, we pay a heavy cost in feelings of guilt and in being *shamed* by our associates when our moral standards vary from one situation to another.

In Japan, just as truly as with us, the various roles we all must play often come into conflict. The difference is that they have an in-bred rationale for justifying the conflicts, as we do not. For example, Japan never lacked for a flow of eager volunteers for kamikasi duty, even though dying for the Emperor meant leaving a family destitute back home. But let us spell out the traditional Shinto code a bit more in detail.

> *Jin* means the ordinary courtesies due to strangers, and general
>   conduct in dealing with the public. Our rough equivalent
>   for it would be "decorum."

---

*Of course I am describing the "old" not the "new" Japan; but the complete culture-imposed discipline evidenced after the surrender in 1945 clearly indicated societal values very different from those of the Western world. The "new" Japan inevitably derives from and incorporates the "old"—just as Puritanism remains a part of our contemporary American character.

*Our own American method of "shifting roles"—less standardized, more unconscious, than among the Japanese—is well described by Erving Goffman: *The Presentation of the Self in Everyday Life,* Doubleday Anchor, 1959; and Talcott Parsons: *The Social System,* Free Press, Glencoe, Illinois, 1951.

Giri means keeping faith in private life—payment of debts, being respectful to superiors; being a good workman: much
of what we comprise in the phrase, "being a good citizen."

Ko means duty to one's own family, in a careful system of
gradation: first to parents, then to sons, then wife, then
daughters. The gradations are inflexible, so there is no
question about divorcing a wife—especially if she is well
loved—if one's mother wishes it; no question about selling
a daughter into prostitution so a son may go to college.

Chu is the most inclusive and takes precedence over all others.
In a phrase, it means being loyal to the Emperor; but since
this also means being loyal to God, it involves the leading of
a generally moral life and the maintenance of self-dignity.
When *chu* has been violated (even unintentionally, or
against one's own will) suicide is the only suitable peni-
tence.

Just as *ko* has its own systematic pattern of gradation, so do
the four circles in relation to one another. One should meet the
demands of *jin* (decorum), until it conflicts with *giri* (citizen-
ship); of *giri* until it interferes with *ko* (family responsibilities);
and all of them, of course, yield to *chu* (loyalty to the Emperor).
Seldom is there an occasion on which the devout Japanese has to
ask himself, "What, in this circumstance, is the right thing to do."
When the codes conflict, the one having higher precedence is the
one that rules. In this kind of society, the supreme personal value
is not individuality, surely not rebelliousness, but obedience and
conformity. Under Shintoism, the supreme task of life is not "the
pursuit of happiness," but the fulfilling of obligations.

To an extent that seems incredible to us, the life of the devout
Japanese is governed by pre-established codes. From early child-
hood he devotes himself to the study of *koan*—a series of 1,700
problems, so difficult that seven years may be required for the
solution of just one of them. Two samples will indicate their nature: "to feel yearning for one's mother before one's conception";
"to conceive the clapping of one hand." *The real lesson is that the
individual is not by himself capable of solving the problems of life.*
The greatest weapon with which society enforces its regulations is
haji, or the shame that results from violating conformity. Loss of

face (another translation for *haji*) results from failure to have done what the relevant code or moral circle demands. The chief motive power of the society is *muga,* which means the doing of what should or must be done with complete effortlessness, complete unselfconsciousness. One's own desires are submerged in the deed itself. For them, self-preservation is *not* the first law of nature; the preservation of self is the denial of *muga.* The advice Japanese youngsters receive is to "live as though already dead." If you yourself were not involved in the situation to the slightest degree, what should be done? This teaching denies what we call conscience, in its place substituting a predetermined and sometimes inscrutable "social good." The important fact is that the individual doesn't have to make up his own mind; it has been made up for him by the code enshrined in the four circles.

Let us shift to a people who are more like ourselves—the Russians.* Foreign observers often comment that no two peoples are more alike than the Russians and the Americans: both exuberant, ambitious, demanding, expansive, self-willed. Yet between Communism and Democracy there seems to be an unbridgeable gulf. In one sense, it really is unbridgeable. For while we teach that truth is relative and is to be discovered through free inquiry, with the majority vote to render the final verdict, Communism is based on the Marxian dialectic which professes to declare what truth is. It has already been discovered and announced. There is no room or reason for debate. A convinced Communist would no more debate the trend of history than you and I would debate the distance from Chicago to Boston. Of course the dialectic was revised somewhat by Lenin and perhaps again in some degree by Khrushchev; but in each instance the truth is stated with final authority, not subject to the give-and-haul of discussion or debate. Parenthetically, it is intriguing now to watch the conflict between the interpretations offered by Khrushchev and Mao Tse-tung; but, again, these are simply two authoritative versions—one or the other

---

*Much this same point was made in an article that appeared just as this book was going to press—Baron Taylor of Harlow: "Deep Analysis of the Russian Mind," *New York Times Magazine,* January 7, 1962, pp. 9, 74-79.

of which will have to prevail. The situation is comparable to the time when the Catholic church had two popes.

If truth is known and defined, there is no room for compromise; concessions are immoral. The goal to be arrived at is immutable. But the route of getting to the goal may be endlessly devious. As Lenin declared, when he spelled out his zig-zag theory of tactics, it is not only permissible but actually necessary for Communists to pretend to compromise, pretend to make concessions—even to sign agreements, so long as they are determined not to keep them. Joseph Stalin made explicit the Communist attitude toward negotiation when he said: "Good words are a mask for evil deeds. Sincere diplomacy is no more possible than iron wood." Senator Karl Mundt, on "Reporters' Round-Up," March 15, 1951, said something that is somewhat similar—but significantly different: "I think, from the standpoint of propaganda, that so long as we are not in a shooting war against a country we should continue to tell the truth. Once you're involved in a war, then you get into the field of psychological warfare, where everything goes that helps to win the conflict." What, then, are we to think of Communist morality? Is this still another unbridgeable gulf between them and us— a genuine difference in moral standards?

I do not think so. In my observation, Communist morality is much like ours. They can tell the difference between the truth and a lie just as well as we can, and they bring the same kind of judgment to bear upon each. Why, then, do they have a long record of deception and untrustworthiness? Let us apply our own standards of morality to what they do, and see what results.

Imagine an incident in the Korean War in which a young American lieutenant concealed a tank in a Korean hut and stationed his men behind stone fences, while a few of them, dressed in the white Korean robes, lolled carelessly around the street. To a column of Communist soldiers which was approaching, the little village appeared to be an undefended haven of peace. When the enemy was within close range, the lieutenant gave the order to fire and cut them down. This was deception—and because it was successful, he got a medal. We all, I am sure, remember another incident from

World War II, just before the allied invasion of North Africa. The British intelligence agents planted a drowned body on the Mediterranean coast, with coded papers in the pockets indicating falsely where the invasion was to occur. The Germans were misled, and the landing was made successfully at another location. Once again, a deliberate lie had served our side well.

But this, of course, was war! In war it is different. In war we ought to do everything we can to confuse and deceive and mislead the enemy in order to win and to do it with the smallest possible loss of life. Precisely so. And precisely so do the Communists reason. The difference—and it is a vast difference—is that in our view war and peace are opposite and alternating conditions; whereas, to the Communist, warfare is perpetual between his system and ours, until, as Khrushchev has observed, they "bury us."

Communism, then, has its own rhetorical principles (based on its different view of the nature of truth) and its own rhetorical methods (based on its view of what we may term the audience situation).

The end, of course, is not yet. The differences that exist around the world are multitudinous. Why, for example, does Nehru appear to be so indifferent to the relative merits of Communist and free world actions? Why does he seem to feel that one side is not much better than another? There are, of course, many explanations arising from his own background—from his dislike of Englishmen and Americans and his own youthful addiction to Communism, for example. From my own experiences with Indian leaders and intellectuals, I do not think the situation would change if Nehru were to be replaced by another capable Hindu. For the views he holds are deeply imbedded in the Indian psyche—a basic derivative from Hinduism and Buddhism.

The problem of good and evil bothers us Judeo-Christians a great deal, for we find it hard to explain how evil exists in a universe created and governed by a God who is all-wise, all-good, and all-powerful. To the Hindu the problem is simple: God created the world by sacrificing his own unity, by breaking himself apart into multitudinality. What is evil is separateness—apartness; what is good is the re-establishment of unity—of getting everything back together once again. Of course this interpretation of Mr. Nehru is far too simple. He is a product not alone of the East but also of an English education. He is willing to fight to protect his own territory. But, then, neither do we Christians practice everything we preach. We believe a great many things about brotherly love and forgiveness of enemies that we feel are absolutely and eternally true, but that often are inconvenient to put into effect. As one Hindu friend of mine phrased it, "You Christians pray in Church on Sunday and on one another during the week." No one practices everything he believes; but we are most apt to practice our genuine beliefs when our own self-interest is not directly involved. And this Mr. Nehru illustrates time and again.

The same kind of problem exists, each time in a different form, as we move from one society to another. Throughout Latin America, for example, Americans have been active in business and diplomacy for many years. Our dollars are welcome, but we ourselves seem to be less well-liked than are, say, the English and the French. One reason is that we insist, more than do the Europeans, on taking our own methods with us. We scorn the siesta and the leisurely approach to business over a cup of tea. We have developed standardized and generally superior methods of packaging our goods (and our ideas) and we don't see any reason to change.

Many a time in the Orient I have observed much the same attitude. Americans who serve out there insist on being comfortable, even luxurious. We live in the best houses and ride around in the best automobiles. We discourage inter-racial marriage. And, we speak our own language. The Russians, on the contrary, send representatives who are trained in the language of the country and who have studied its customs. They live unobtrusively in native-style huts and are encouraged to marry women of the country. In other words, they try to deal with the people according to the standards of those people; and we find their success disheartening to our cause.

The examples could be extended through Africa and the Mohammedan Middle East. Every culture has, to some degree, its own rhetoric—often very different from our own. We can't learn them all—though I see no reason why we can't train specialists in each. As a Speech profession, however, there are some things we can do.

We can ally our discipline (our study and our teaching) much more closely with cultural anthropology, social psychology, and general linguistics.

We can remind ourselves when we deal with other peoples that in practically all cultures different from our own, ceremonialism and ritual are far more important than they are with us. The reason, I think, is a simple one. Amidst our richness of opportunities, it is not easy to fail, and the emphasis is upon getting things done. In more impoverished societies, it is not easy to accomplish very much; and this makes more important the manner of the doing.

Finally, we can stop teaching our students *a* mode of rhetoric and instead teach them the heart of the rhetorical process—which, I take it, is to discover not so much *what* other people think as *how* they formulate their ideas.

We often hear that travel is broadening. It is questionable whether this is really true. On the contrary, it seems that for most people travel is actually narrowing. The further they get from Dubuque, the more Dubuque appeals to them. What we need is to learn to look for the values and standards of value of the people among whom we move—if not to adopt them, at least to understand, to appreciate, to learn how to deal with them.

Let us conclude with a reminder from the youth of Patrick Henry. Henry taught himself to be an effective speaker not so much by speaking as by listening. As a youthful store-keeper, he failed in business largely because he converted his store into a debate and discussion club. He encouraged all manner of idlers to sit around and talk, while he said nothing except to stimulate the discussion with a question or a challenge when the talk lagged. What he was doing was listening—not listening to find out what idlers thought (for generally they knew no more than he did about the subjects of the discourse) but to find out *how* they thought—what impelled them toward some conclusions and away from others. So fascinating was this observation that he simply refused to be a merchant. The story is that one day as he lay on a sack of salt listening with rapt attention to a group of talkers, a customer came in asking for salt. "Sorry!" Henry snapped. "Just sold the last peck." Naturally, he failed in business; but he learned things about human motivation that laid the foundation for his transcendent abilities on the platform.

What we need is what Patrick Henry needed—to learn all we can about how other people, in other cultural groups, think. What we need is an awareness of other rhetorics—so far as we can get it, a detailed understanding of at least some of them. The mere recognition that such a need exists is a small start in the right direction.

Chapter 8

THE TOP COMMUNIST WEAPON—
THE SPOKEN WORD

WHEN NIKITA KHRUSHCHEV says to the Western democratic nations, "We will bury you," then adds a bit later that the Soviet Union does not want a shooting war, he is not necessarily contradicting himself. Marxism is based upon *dialectical* materialism, which means that in the opinion of its followers it is a logical necessity. Marx believed that the free capitalistic system carries within itself the seeds of its own destruction and must therefore *inevitably* destroy itself. There is no doubt faith enough yet remaining among the orthodox Communists to give them a hope, however vaguely defined, that victory will come to them by default. Beyond this, however, there lies a conviction not unlike that which leads Christians to sacrifice and work in order that God's plan for mankind may the sooner and the more surely come to fruition. What must be must be—but true believers nevertheless should exercise skill, diligence, and faithful self-sacrifice in doing those things which will directly contribute to the expected result. Hot warfare is by no means ruled out by the Communist strategists—as witness the various attacks on neighboring states launched by the Red Chinese, the attack on the Republic of Korea, and the Russian suppression of the Hungarian revolt. The principal weapons directed against the free world, however, are drawn from the bountiful arsenal of rhetoric. Brain-washing, subversion, propaganda, and a perverted form of group discussion have proved of far more value to Communism than have its massed armies and modern missiles. Persuasion as we have known it traditionally flourishes best in free forums where honest opinions may be swayed by the weight of argument; but Communism has introduced a rhetoric of another sort, designed for other ends.

In preceding chapters, where it has been necessary to refer to the rhetoric of Communism, the point has been made that Communists believe it is wrong for them to permit their judgment to be affected by any pronouncements or factual accounts except those which come to them from an approved source. In this particular, they are like orthodox religious sects. *The Devil knows how to quote Scripture for his purpose,* we are warned. We should not, then, listen to what may be said by those outside our own faith, no matter how true or how appealing it may sound, for it is contaminated with evil. The prevalence of this view in some segments of Christianity should make it easier for us to understand how in all sincerity a similar view may be and is held by even intelligent and well-informed Communists. Even the evidence of the senses must be repudiated if it conflicts with the truth that is promulgated by official and approved sources. This belief is one of the strong Communist barriers against persuasion from democratic sources which is directed toward the peoples behind the Iron and Bamboo Curtains.

In accord with this trust in their own exponents of their own orthodoxy is a staunch faith that essential and unvarying truth has been unquestionably determined by the principal prophets of Marxism. The effects of this faith were well expressed by H. M. Spitzer, at a "Washington Conference on International Communication," held on January 4, 1956. "The Western attitude," Mr. Spitzer reminded us, "is rooted in the feeling that, as a general rule, the minority should acquiesce in the will of the majority—an attitude that can be shared by a minority that has reason to hope that someday enough of the majority may become convinced of the minority view and join them to form a new majority. This attitude rests on the feeling that every man has as good a chance of hitting on the truth as his neighbor and that certainty is unattainable." In other words, in our democratic conception we deal at best with probabilities and these are argued out in free assemblies where the best arguments in the long run tend to prevail. Minorities favor free discussion for their own benefit and majorities agree (sometimes half-heartedly) because through the unfettered ballot box they will doubtless someday find themselves reduced to a minority position.

"Now this feeling is not shared by the Russians who are Communists," Mr. Spitzer continued, "and who not only believe that certainty is attainable but are convinced that it has been attained by their leaders who are trained in the method of Marxist analysis. Since this is their belief, they would act irrationally if they permitted their findings to be set aside by a majority decision, and fail in their duty if they did not apply every available means—including coercion—to make their views prevail."

The distinctive attribute of Communist rhetoric is not faith in the infallibility of their doctrines; for this same faith has been held by many followers of many beliefs. Neither is the Communist tendency to make their views prevail by force or by deception unique. The special characteristic of Communist rhetoric is that it does not put persuasion in one category and coercion in another; it combines them. The Communist leadership long ago reached the conclusion that men must be cowed by fear while at the same time being animated by hope; and while their minds are distraught by this combination of contraries, their opinions can and must be changed. They believe the change can be accomplished in a manner to make it fundamental and lasting. It is this process to which Edward Hunter first gave the name "brain-washing," in his 1951 book, *Brain-Washing in Red China*. The process came under the scrutiny of Western scholars after the Communist conquest of China, when it was used upon American and English prisoners. But it had proved its effectiveness as early as 1936-37, when Lavrenti Beria, and Andrei Vishinsky, Stalin's Chief of the Secret Police and Chief Prosecutor, used it to secure a series of "confessions" from Russian Communist deviationists who were marked for execution. At that time Western observers concluded that the victims were weakened by torture then forced to agree to fabricated confessions to save the lives of their families. Even so, the abjectness and apparent sincerity of their insistence on their own guilt, when in the open courtroom, was bewildering. There was a tendency to explain it as a peculiarity of the Slavic temperament. Then, in 1950, the same results appeared in Western captives of both Russian and Chinese Communists. The bodies of these victims did not show marks of physical torture. But their minds and personalities were deeply and lastingly changed.

Robert A. Vogeler, an American businessman who in a Budapest trial confessed to spying, was one of the first Westerners to come to public attention after suffering the brain-washing ordeal. After seventeen months of imprisonment, he was released and gradually regained the power to remember, evaluate, and relate his experiences. One of his striking memories was the boast of a member of the interrogation team: "If God Himself was sitting in that chair we would make him say what we wanted him to say." Vogeler's health was undermined by solitary confinement in cold, dark cells, and by lack of food and medical care. But the most startling effects were his doubt of his own innocence and his feeling that his captors had treated him fairly and with justice. He had been subjected to a new and fearful system of persuasion.

Before many months had passed, means were developed for applying this same brain-washing technique upon masses of men simultaneously. The first mass victims were thousands of Japanese Prisoners-of-War, held by the Russians for several years after the end of World War II. When they finally were returned home, many of them came back as convinced Communists. Whatever the system was, it worked. During and after the Korean War, numerous Americans were subjected to it, and gradually the details of the brain-washing technique have come to light.

The methods used are those identified in the experiments of Pavlov—the weakening of the body and the will through cold, solitude, lack of sufficient food, deprivation of all sympathetic human comradeship, and a seemingly senseless alternation of rewards and punishments, based on no pattern of rational predictability. The results sought (and sometimes achieved) are to imbue the victims with a lasting belief in the infallible truth of the Communist doctrines, and especially in the doctrine that they must believe what the orthodoxy of the system dictates, regardless of the evidence of their senses or their own power of reason.

The Sunday New York *Times* for February 26, 1955, carried a story of two Americans, a man and a woman, who had returned home after three and a half years of imprisonment in Red China, on charges of spying. They insisted they had deserved their punishment, that they had been well treated, and that the Communist system is so much superior to free enterprise that it will be adopted around the world.

During that same week, there appeared on the newsstands an issue of *Look,* containing an article, "Inside Red China," by William Stevenson. In it this Canadian reporter relates how he was escorted through Communist China with glowing assurances that everything was wonderful in "the workers' paradise." After enjoying the opera in Shanghai, he went back-stage to congratulate the singers. Then, suddenly, he "saw the naked reality behind the Bamboo Curtain." There on a prominently displayed blackboard was written an abject "confession" of error by one of the singers. As Stevenson wrote, "He had uttered some criticism of the government. The Communist cell in the theatre called a discussion meeting. His fellow thespians recited his weaknesses and sins. Now it was all there on the blackboard, retold by the miserable wretch himself."

What had happened to the two Americans, they would not reveal. But the case of the Shanghai opera singer indicated an extension of the brain-washing technique in two dimensions: (1) it was being applied broadly to the whole population of China, not to just a few imprisoned captives; and (2) it was being inflicted upon the people by themselves, not just by a corps of skilled experts. Obviously, a big "leap forward," a "major break-through" (to borrow two favorite Communist cliches), had been achieved in the use of their own peculiar form of rhetoric. Close to the heart of this new method is the extensive use of small group discussions.

An introduction to the use of the discussion techniques is found in a book of wartime experiences, *The Jungle is Neutral* (1953), by an Englishman, F. Chapman, who described his two years of guerrilla activities in World War II behind the Japanese lines in the Malayan jungles. The life was one of incredible hardship, in which his companions were a group of Communist Chinese. Most of the book deals with their hunger, suffering, and danger. But even in the midst of their travail, scarcely a day passed without a two or three hour lecture-discussion on the Marxian doctrines of history and their bearing on the current conflict. As a highly educated Englishman, Chapman was amazed at the thoroughness of the indoctrination program, which persisted without a break even during the torrential rains and amidst the discomforts of the malarial swamplands.

During the Korean War, well-trained Allied interrogators interviewed thousands of North Korean refugees who had fled into southern Korea. They all related stories of forced attendance at weekly discussion meetings, and most of them exhibited a relatively similar reaction. In these meetings they were told and were forced to repeat a great deal about the glories of Communism which they did not believe, for their daily experience proved it to be lies. But what they were told about the hatefulness of American imperialism they did not seriously question—for the charges were always buttressed with many alleged facts, and they never had opportunity to encounter any refutation. The North Koreans who fled southward were tough-minded and rebellious against the Reds, as was indicated by their abandonment of their homes and friends in order to seek freedom. Yet even these had suffered deeply inflicted mental wounds and twisted thinking, all the more invidious because it had been imposed on them from within their own misdirected brains.

It had become apparent that the weapons of Communism are not alone guns and bombs, nor torture and slave-labor camps. Their arsenal of weapons directed against their own people and the outside world include also tortured ideas and a lethal misuse of facts. The rhetoric of Communism became a subject the free world will have to master if democracy is to survive.

We of the democratic West are accustomed to thinking of public speaking, debate, and discussion—and particularly discussion—as essential instruments of democracy. It is therefore somewhat shocking for us to discover that in recent years they have been adapted and utilized as indispensable weapons of Communist tyranny. The fact is that the Communists have taken over our most typical methodology of free government and have twisted and distorted it to fit their own totalitarian purposes.

Our early New England forebears developed the town meeting as the fundamental creative source of self-government. In these meetings the townspeople gathered to exchange opinions on use of

the common grazing lands, the laying out of streets, and the establishment of schools. A moderator presided with no more power
than was required to maintain orderliness in considering the problems, and every member had an equal voice and an equal vote.
The process represents democracy in its ultimate purity. Yet by a
skilled perversion of the process at its most crucial points, the
Communists perverted it into an instrument of tyranny.

The basis for this transformation lies in the Communist link-
age of persuasion and terror. Mental control is what they sought,
but this they could achieve only within the framework of physical
control. Two factors were essential for what they sought (and
seek) to achieve: first, that the people with whom they deal must
be aware of the helplessness and defencelessness of their position
under their domination by ruthlessly cold-blooded masters; and,
second, that the right words must be spoken by the right people in
the right way. In differing areas these two essential factors have
been adapted in both form and substance to local conditions. But
both are always present. Without the intertwining of the two,
mass brain-washing would be an impossibility.

The crude but effective basic pattern was worked out by Nickolai Lenin, the chief architect of Marxian dictatorship. Lenin
was tireless in hammering home to his lieutenants the theme that
dictatorship can succeed in the long run only as it remains "close
to the mass of the people." This closeness of contact he achieved
by two supplementary means: by establishing a vast network of
secret espionage directed against his own people, with rewards for
those who would report any deviationist acts or words by their
friends, family, or neighbors, and with instant and ruthless punishment for all of whom there was "reasonable doubt" that they might
be guilty; and by establishing concurrently a system of enforced
attendance at weekly or even semi-weekly small discussion meetings. The pattern was simple: death or slave labor if you failed to
think, say, and do what the dictatorship demanded, combined with
frequent occasions for thinking, saying, and doing whatever the
dictatorship prescribed.

In the years since Lenin's death, this system has been altered in
some details by Stalin, Khrushchev, Mao Tze-tung and other Com-

munist leaders, depending on external circumstances and the nature of the populations with which they have dealt. But the intermingling of terror and persuasion remains the central core.

In North Korea, for example, after the establishment of the Communist control in the fall of 1945, the three and a half per cent of the population identified as landlords were ruthlessly liquidated. Then farm tenancy was "abolished." In its place, all farm land was declared to be the common property of the State—belonging alike to all the people. Distribution of the land to the farmers who must cultivate it was accomplished by local Communist Central Committees, who granted acreage lots to farm families that were found to be dependably loyal. In order to prove their loyalty, and thus receive land, the young people joined the Communist Youth Corps, the adults attended semi-weekly discussion meetings, the whole family participated in frequent mass meetings and demonstrations, and all able-bodied men and women gave freely of their time to assigned public works projects, such as building roads, clearing swamps, building irrigation systems, and the like. Titles of occupancy of the land were for one year only and were always subject to instant cancellation. In order to maintain occupancy, the families had to prove their constant devotion to the regime by word and deed. Meanwhile, the best means of getting more or better land was to inform the authorities of suspicious behavior by those whose lands the informers coveted. Mutual suspicion within neighborhoods and even within families was thereby fostered by self-interest, while independence and self-respect were undermined by the absolute dependence of all upon the whim of the Communist Committees. Meanwhile, desperation was further induced by heavy taxation that took everything except the barest means of subsistence.

In China Mao Tze-tung proceeded first along the same lines, then went on to the further step of breaking up the family structure by establishing huge communes, with common cultivation of the fields and with common dormitories and dining halls. Children were separted from their parents, to be cared for in State nurseries and kindergartens, leaving both parents free for work. Older sons and daughters were organized into Youth Corps, which were shifted about from one area to another to labor on State projects. Whatever time was left over from work was requisitioned for mass rallies and for small discussion meetings.

In these meetings, speech is not free but it is decidedly frequent. In essence the meetings resemble the "confessional" prayer meetings that used to be a common feature of our own rural churches. In these meetings the members were encouraged to rise regularly to "confess their sins" and to ask the understanding aid of their neighbors in achieving a better mode of life. In the Communist meetings, this self-confessional is supplemented by the practice of having members gently but firmly point out deviationist behavior by their neighbors. Since the group is small and is composed of people who live and work together, everyone knows a great deal about the others. Failure to attend a mass rally, or even a look or a gesture of seeming dissent, attracts instant attention and becomes a subject for searching examination in the meetings. The suspected member only heightens suspicion if he denies any intent of guilt. His only safe procedure is to rise to his feet and confess that selfishness or ignorance led him momentarily astray, then to promise that he will make extra efforts hereafter to compensate for his faults.

In a different pattern, the meetings also serve an instructional purpose. Leaders outline new directives that have been received and make sure all understand them. Then earnest efforts are made to induce every possible criticism of them. An atmosphere of permissiveness and apparent fairness is generated. The leader declares earnestly that he fully realizes these new directives will invoke special hardships on this community. He points out that the policies have to be devised for the nation as a whole, and that local conditions make some of them unsuitable for this area. He urges everyone to suggest any possible changes or ameliorations that ought to be adopted in terms of local or individual needs. When a member hesitantly indicates that his own family circumstances will suffer through these policies, his contribution is welcomed and agreed with. Others are thereby encouraged to state the basis for any objections or reservations they may have. The aim of this portion of the meeting is to discover as fully as possible every form of dissatisfaction with the new policies.

Then the discussion shifts to the necessity for the proposed programs. The point is made unavoidably clear that they will have to be put into effect, regardless of what hardships they may cause. Members are encouraged to stand up and assert their wholehearted determination to do their part in carrying them out, despite the personal cost. Everyone who has uttered a complaint is especially under the pressure of the combined group opinion to make his own declaration of support particularly strong. The meeting does not adjourn until the last dissident has fully endorsed what is to be done. If there is a lingering hesitancy on the part of one or more, the leader adopts a stern tone and warns that lack of cooperation will not be tolerated. The power of the police hovers like a heavy shadow over the meeting and will be invoked if there is any prolonged reluctance. Any member who frequently objects or who is often slow in his final agreement is likely to disappear from his home at night. Terror is always the backdrop; but the goal is to achieve the fullest and readiest possible display of willing and even eager compliance.

In present day Russia the terror is diminished, in part because the pattern of basic compliance has become firmly fixed in the whole social structure. Much greater leeway is now possible than in China for expressions of dissent and for independence of judgment. The police power has become considerably curbed, with open court trials replacing secret midnight arrests. Yet the fact is fully understood that the greater freedom results from the mutual forebearance by the citizenry on the one hand and the State on the other. Punishment for deviationism is now less likely to be exile to Siberia; it may, rather, be shifting the critic to a less desirable job or apartment, or the deprivation of vacation privileges, or manifestations of disfavor by the authorities, resulting in avoidance of the offender by his former friends. But greater power remains to be used when and if needed. And there are no signs that the general compliance of the people with the policies of the State is in any way weakened. Virtual unanimity of opinion and conformity of behavior remains the hallmark of even the "liberal-ized" Soviet community.

Unsophisticated Western visitors in Communist countries may be misled as they observe what seems to be happening in these Communist discussions. They may hear arguments that develop with considerable heat, and they see members rise boldly to disagree with what the leader has said. Finally, they observe the meeting concluded with a common agreement on the points at issue; and they may feel that this is just what happens when sound discussion techniques are followed in meetings within the democracies. What they have really observed is the form, without attaining to an understanding of the real nature of what happens. But the Communists themselves are in no doubt as to what is taking place.

The chief psychological superiority of speech as a means of social control is the immediacy of its two-way communication. Speaker and audience confront one another. The earnestness, conversational directness, and apparent sincerity of the speaker lends credibility to his words. The doubts and perplexities of the listeners are open to the perception of the speaker, who can proceed instantly to answer their questions. No more effective mode of influence has ever been found. To make effective use of it requires a tremendous apparatus of organization; and the Communists have not hesitated to devote the necessary effort to developing this crucial weapon in their arsenal of psychological warfare.

From the very early days of its first great success in conquering Russia, the Communist International has recognized and implemented the revolutionary values of controlled public discussion. The Second World Congress of the Communist International assembled in Moscow from July 17 to August 7, 1920. It adopted a set of theses which clearly spelled out both the repudiation of free speech and the determination to make use of its distorted forms.

Among the resolutions adopted were the following: "Communism repudiates parliamentarianism as the form of the future; . . . . it repudiates the possibility of winning over parliaments; its aim is to destroy parliamentarianism." Then comes the vital principle. Communist Party members are commanded to seek membership in free organizations within the non-Communist nations, "in order to direct the masses to blow up the whole bourgeois machinery and the parliament itself from within . . . . This work within the parliaments . . . consists chiefly in making revolutionary propaganda from the parliamentary platform." Anyone who misses the point of Communist activity in the United Nations is simply refusing to take seriously the most sober declarations adopted by the Party itself.

In this 1920 set of theses, the role of Communist members in free national legislatures was sharply defined: "The regular proposing of demonstrative measures, not for the purpose of having them passed by the bourgeois majority, but for the purposes of propaganda, agitation, and organization . . . . . Each Communist representative must remember he is not a 'legislator,' who is bound to seek agreement with other legislators, but an agitator of the Party, detailed into the enemy's camp in order to carry out the orders of the Party there."

Emphasizing the revolutionary effectiveness of controlled speech that is misrepresented as being free, the resolutions adopted by the Second Congress of the Communist International continue: "The rank-and-file Communist worker must not shrink from speaking in the bourgeois parliaments, and not give way to the so-called experienced parliamentarians, even if such workmen are novices in parliamentary methods. In case of need the workmen representatives may read their speeches from notes, in order that the speech may be printed afterwards in the papers or in leaflet form."

Aside from the crassly clear statement of the purpose of their membership and speaking activities in free organizations, what chiefly emerges from these directions is the thoroughness and detail of the organization. The same thoroughness is apparent in the discussion programs carried on inside the Communist countries.

The Communists spare neither time, energy, or money in the recruitment, training, and control of the speakers (or *agitators,* as they are called) who address students in the schools, workmen attending indoctrination lectures in the factories, and villagers attending the required discussion meetings. In February, 1946, within the Soviet Union itself there were enrolled approximately three million such agitators. This means one for each 100 of the population—or one for every 65 persons fifteen years of age or older. In addition, larger numbers were recruited for special occasions, such as election campaigns.

In the Ukraine Republic, in 1949, there were enrolled 764,000 such agitators, or one for every 50 persons. Moscow, with a population of five million, had 160,000 agitators in 1946, or one for every 30 inhabitants.

This is a principal means by which the Party has obeyed the injunction of Lenin and Stalin to "stay close to the masses." Agitators are assigned special groups or areas, with which they are in daily intimate contact, so that they can deliver the Party messages with shrewd insight into the needs and problems of the group. Each lecture is thereby rendered "audience-centered" in its content. Every speech is followed by a question-forum discussion, to insure that the speaker's point is clearly understood and that all doubts and objections are immediately ferreted out and countered.

But while the speaker is close to his audience on the one hand, a fortnightly *Agitator's Handbook* is provided to keep him also well informed of the precise "Party line" formulated in headquarters, which he is expected to propound. In addition to facts and Party policy pronouncements, this guide contains advice on how to answer typical objections and how to interpret policy reversals that appear to be inconsistent with previous directives.

The *Agitator's Handbook* has the largest circulation of any periodical within the Soviet Union. Between 1925 and 1939 its circulation multiplied eighteen times, and in the next four years (during the German invasion) its circulation again multiplied four-fold. By 1947 it was translated into nine non-Russian languages, with a total circulation of 800,000. This indicates the minimum number of agitators then conducting discussion meetings.

The agitators are selected from volunteers who have been cleared for their loyalty and ability by the local Communist Committees. After recruitment, the speakers are sent to speech seminars known as *Agit-Kollectives,* which were first established in 1923. In 1938 a set of "Model Rules for Agit-Kollectivs" was adopted. They comprise a highly selective set of rhetorical principles, fully as pragmatic as Aristotle's *Rhetoric*, but far more explicitly prescriptive. Speakers are not permitted to develop any basic ideas of their own, but are encouraged to devise examples and references to experience that will fit the habits of thought of the particular audience they know so intimately.

After initial training, the agitators are required to continue meeting in the Agit-Kollectiv every ten days, to learn precise methods of presenting specific policies and to secure guidance on how to counter typical objections and queries. Each agitator reports on reactions from his own audience. The most effective methods of the best agitators are published in the *Agitator's Handbook* for the guidance of all. The key advice they receive is: "Do not hide from a puzzling, trenchant, or even hostile question, but, on the contrary, give an answer that is straightforward and full of the stuff of the Party spirit."

In Red China this same system is followed, but with even more thoroughness and with additional emphasis upon such publicity media as billboards, parades, exhibits, and lavish use of street-corner loud-speakers. In a book called *The Communist Persuasion* (1959), written by a Catholic priest, Eleutherius Winance, after living for three years under Communist Chinese rule, the essence of the Communist psychology of persuasion is identified as comprising five factors. First, the general appeals are always to idealism—sacrifice, loyalty, brotherhood—and against the self-seeking ego. Second, an all-pervasive unanimity of expressed opinion is achieved by means of rigid censorship, governmental dominance of all opinion-organs, and encouragement of children to report even the slightest deviationist sentiments expressed within the family. Third, an incredibly massive and minute persuasive campaign is maintained, including a constant barrage of public propaganda and compulsory attendance by everyone in three four-hour "confessional" discussions each week. Fourth, the self-trust of individuals is systematically broken down by emphasis on the need for repetitive self-denunciation and purgative confessions of error. Finally, behind the persuasion is the ruthless employment of force and terror, with slave labor or death the only alternatives for those who do not conform. Basic to this system is the Communist conviction that no one is strong enough to stand against what every one says—especially when he himself must join in the saying of it.

At the United Nations, and in many post-World War II conferences, Allied representatives have had ample opportunity to learn the Communist techniques for international negotiation. A collection of commentaries by such participants has been published by Raymond Dennett and Joseph Johnson, in a 1951 volume entitled *Negotiating with the Russians.* In 1955, Vice-Admiral C. Turner Joy, who conducted the negotiations with the Communists at Panmunjom, leading to the Korean Truce, presented the fruits of his experience in a valuable book, *How the Communists Negotiate.* Further revelations are included in a long series of memoirs written by American and British diplomats and national leaders.

From such sources the following sixteen negotiating principles or methods followed by the Communists in international conferences may be identified.

1. Meticulous adherence to Communist doctrinal interpretations.of what must be true of certain types of situations, regardless of the facts of the particular case.

2. Imperturbable persistence in maintaining their position, without regard for factual or logical demonstrations of its falsity.

3. Wearisome and seemingly endless repitition of their arguments, apparently with the aim of wearing down the patience of their opponents.

4. Presentation and defense of an agenda that is composed of the conclusions they wish to reach rather than of the problems to be solved.

5. Definition of terms to suit their own purposes rather than the facts. For example, at Panmunjom when the discussion topic was the possible withdrawal of all foreign troops from Korea, General Nam Il, representing the Communists, defined "foreign troops" as all soldiers brought into Korea with the permission of their own governments. Since the Communists insisted that the Red Chinese troops were all there as "volunteers," he declared that

the United Nations forces were foreign, but the Red Chinese were not.

6. Creation of *incidents,* such as the charges of U. N. bombing of targets within the conference area, as a means of influencing the course of the negotiations.

7. Complete control of decision-making concerning their own policies from headquarters in Moscow and Peiping, so that their representatives had power to accept concessions but no power to make any.

8. Prolonged delay, including boycotts of sessions for periods of many weeks, in the "hope to exploit to their advantage the characteristic impatience of Western peoples."

9. Vitriolic abuse of the opposing negotiators, in an effort to arouse displays of temper which could be cited as reasons for failure to achieve agreement.

10. Publicity of any and all phases of the discussions which could be represented as favorable to their side—despite agreements to limit publicity to joint statements signed by both sides.

11. Insistence upon inserting into the agreements statements that are worded ambiguously, to facilitate whatever later interpretations may suit their purposes.

12. The introduction of spurious or irrelevant issues to be used as bargaining points. This often consists of making a series of outrageous demands, from which they later withdraw with the claim that they are making a series of concessions which the Allied nations must match with genuine concessions on germaine issues.

13. Insistence upon a veto provision governing all the machinery for effectuating whatever agreements may be reached. This has become the bedrock of Khrushchev's program for any or all negotiations with the West.

14. A rationalistic distortion of facts, consisting of selecting "out of the whole truth certain parts, which, when put together in a particular way, produce a conclusion exactly contradictory to the whole truth."

15. Repudiation of agreements that have been reached, through the medium of "re-interpreting" them. Even if great care had been

taken to formulate the agreements in terms of meticulous precision, the claim is made that later events have changed the context and therefore the meaning.

16. Utilization of their most capable and intelligent members as spokesmen, regardless to their rank, while the real head of the delegation may remain speechless and sometimes even unidentified in the background—but always available to signal the spokesman when he approaches the limit of his authority.

From the factors discussed in this chapter it is evident that the Communists have developed an elaborate theory of persuasion based upon the use of terror when dealing with peoples under their own control and the use of deception (or what Lenin called "zig-zag tactics") when dealing with other peoples and governments. It is also clear that they regard propaganda, negotiation, and participation in free world organizations as enormously important instruments for their program of seeking global domination. Although the democracies have long stressed the values of discussion, the Communists far exceed us in the efforts they make to organize and conduct discussion groups. In order to provide uniformity of guidance from their centralized power centers for their far-flung network of propagandists, they must perforce publish both their intentions and their methods. If we persist in regarding their conduct as "mysterious," it is simply because we refrain from taking the trouble to analyze or interpret what they do —or even what they tell us they are doing. Our most crucial international problems consist of our dealings with Communism; yet we have been slow to study the nature of Communist rhetoric. If the world is really to be won not by war but by words, this kind of study is urgently needed. The words and the deeds are remarkably consistent. There is no reason why we should let ourselves be further misled.

Chapter 9

PATTERNS OF CONFUCIAN THOUGHT

IT IS LESS THAN five hundred years since the discovery of America by Columbus. It is not much more than five hundred years since the Middle Ages gave way to the Renaissance. It is a century less than five hundred years since Galileo made the first halting steps that ushered in our new age of science. In terms of what can happen to the human race, five hundred years is a long time. It was just over five hundred years before the beginning of the Christian era that a Chinese scholar who lived in genteel poverty in a small province named Chou—a rather crusty schoolteacher who was beloved by no one except a small group of loyal students—a whispy, impractical, unheroic and unimpressive man named Kung Tse-fu introduced a system of thought now known as Confucianism which for five times five hundred years has deeply affected the way of life and manner of thought of more than half the inhabitants of the globe.

The way in which influence is exerted and spreads is a neverending puzzle. In the eighth century a middle-aged Arabian merchant finally, after years of futile persuasion, managed to convert his wife to a new system of ethical-religious ideas, and shortly Mohammedanism was burning its way across the middle of the then-known world. In the twelfth century a white-bearded old hermit named Peter commenced to preach to children about the desirability of seizing the Holy Land from its Muslim inhabitants, and for two hundred years Europe was swept by a frenzy of crusading zeal. Just how such fires of fanatic zeal are set alight is difficult to determine. Apparently there are times when an uneasy spirit of inquietude and dimly-sensed dissatisfaction are exploded by an idea that otherwise might slip through the public mind with scarcely a ripple. The philosophy of Confucianism apparently was something the vast population of the Orient needed and inexplicably it conquered the minds of multiple millions of people who were divided by constant warfare, by differing traditions and social systems, by differences of language, by vast distances broken by high mountains, wide rivers, and empty deserts, and by a lack of either ready means of communication or any precedent for international communicating.

In essence the message taught by Master Kung, or Confucius, as we shall hereafter call him, was very simple. It was first of all a message of personal responsibility and secondly a humbling reminder that there is great wisdom in learning from the experience of preceding generations and especially from the Sages. The Sixth Century B. C. into which Confucius was born was a time of poverty, turmoil, corruption, and all manner of inhumane injustices. China was divided into a multiplicity of little kingdoms, each ruled by a Warlord who ruthlessly exploited his own people and raided his neighbors whenever he dared. The very idea of ethics was a shadowy figment based solely on such loyalties as were demanded by immediate circumstances. Selfishness and force were the standards by which men lived and fought. Complaints were rampant against the misrule of kings and the extortions of landlords. What Confucius said, in effect, was: instead of complaining about the conduct of the great and the powerful whom you cannot influence, why not try to improve your own behavior?

When the heart is purified, he said, the individual leads a better life. As the individual elevates his own standards of conduct, the quality of family life is improved. As families become better ordered, the community is cleansed of many vices. As communities become dependably ethical, the whole nation is more orderly, just, and stable. To enforce this conception of individual-centered responsibility, Confucius devised a moral code known as *Li*, or the five-fold relationships. According to this code, younger children owe affectionate obedience to their elder brothers, all the children to their parents, the wife to her husband, neighbors to neighbors, and citizens to the king. The whole framework was one of subordination, establishing a dependable hierarchy through which orderliness was enforced by the responsibilities imposed on those lower in the scale. Through a spelling out for each person of where his own loyalties were to be directed, ambition and uncertainty were eliminated. Stability rather than progress became the social ideal.

From the instant of birth, the role that each individual would play in various stages of life was clearly defined.

Within this broad general framework, the remaining gaps were easily filled in. Among the vocational groupings that were known to Confucius, soldiers were placed at the bottom of the social scale, then merchants, then farmers, and, at the top, scholars. The absolute power of kings was countered by the declaration that they were chosen by heaven to rule so long as they ruled righteously, with the same responsibility for the welfare of their subjects that parents have for their children. If a king acted tyrannically, the favor of heaven was withdrawn and his subjects were justified (even impelled) to arise in revolt and assist in his replacement with a magnanimous monarch.

Scholars were placed at the top of the hierarchy because it was their business to study the ancient classics in order to learn and to teach the wisdom of the Sages. What one man can learn is far less than what mankind has learned. Thus society benefits as the experience of the past is brought to bear to help solve the problems of the present. Justice was to be the touchstone by which every act was to be evaluated. Return good for good, Confucius taught, for this will encourage goodness; and punish evil with evil, for this will discourage wickedness. Order, system, dependability, and rationality were the great virtues. The rights of individuals were to be cherished and defended—within carefully prescribed limits and according to carefully defined modes.

This was the essence of the teaching of Confucius, whose handful of scholars followed him about in his wanderings with the hungry devotion of men who for the first time were hearing sensible solutions for problems that had heretofore seemed insoluble. Some of his disciples became high officials, with power to impose elements of his code within the government. Confucius himself, after many disappointments, was finally named to a minor office, in which he failed to distinguish himself. The Duke of Chou became interested enough to inquire into the teachings of Confucius, but abandoned them when he found they did not enhance his domestic powers or help him in his wars with neighboring princes.

Nevertheless, the Confucian system spread rapidly among the scholars of the East and with astonishing speed became entrenched as the ruling guide for the widespread agglomeration of peoples who felt themselves to be a part of Chinese civilization.

As we consider how to deal with the Confucian mentality (and, later, with Taoist and Buddhist idea systems) the first necessity is to make sure we understand our own. From this point comparisons may be made and methods of communicating from our own to other cultural patterns may be devised.

Rhetoric is commonly conceived as a pattern of manipulative devices or techniques by which one mind can influence other minds. More basically, rhetoric is itself a mode of thinking. It is the kind of thinking by which we try to determine the *relationships* that exist between the truth of the matter under consideration, the purpose or personal goals of the one doing the considering, and the needs or susceptibilities of those who are to be influenced in their attitude toward the subject. The logician is concerned with the relationships that lie within a subject: if such-and-such is true about it, what else must inevitably follow? The scientific method makes a quite similar inquiry, though it imposes upon the subject certain external disturbances, in order to observe through its re-actions what its intrinsic nature must be. Dialectic is a method of analytic inquiry into the nature of a subject by questioning its various aspects. All these are means of determining *what is true*. Rhetoric is concerned with truth (or what Freud called the Reality Principle) in terms of human purposes. In what sense is it true *for me,* the rhetorician asks; and how can I make it *appear true to these others* whose reactions are important to the accomplishment of my purpose? The father of the rhetoric of the West is Aristotle, and all we have done with it since his time is to make minor modi-fications of emphasis within the framework he discerned.

It is clear that, in Aristotle's view, rhetoric is a way of thinking. Rhetoric has no subject matter of its own, but is a way of dealing with any suitable subject. It is "the faculty of discovering in the particular case all the available means of persuasion."

The subject matter that is amenable to rhetorical inquiry is not as inclusive as that considered by logic, dialectic, and science.

When the sole question to be asked is, "What is true?" this inquiry can be directed to any conceivable subject. But rhetoric is a mode of determining what is true for me and what can be made to appear true for others. Thus it is confined to matters on which there is room for honest doubt. As Aristotle phrased it, "this art has to do with matters that may turn out in more than one way." Its concern is with probabilities rather than certainties. Like ethics, rhetoric deals with variable relationships which may be adjusted, for good or ill, in terms of human desires. The end to be sought is the influencing of an audience.

According to Aristotle, the purpose of the speaker is limited by two factors which lie beyond his own control. The first is the fact that truth and justice are realities; these he cannot deny. In the long run he cannot avoid them; and in immediate circumstances it is his duty to uphold them. The second factor is human nature, which comprises the audience the speaker must address. In Aristotle's view, man is potentially rational, but is very largely governed by emotions. Hence, the speaker can only influence listeners by appealing to their emotions, as well as to their minds. In addition to presenting facts and logic in support of his position, he must represent what he has to say in terms of their own wants and fears. And he will find that their judgment is very greatly influenced by what they think of his own character, reputation, and personality— a combination Aristotle called his *ethos*.

Thus the speaker is confronted in every circumstance with a three-fold task. He must try to accomplish (a) what he himself most desires; (b) what the facts prescribe or at least make possible; and (c) what the audience is desirous or at least capable of receiving. This is the foundation of persuasion as it has been known and advocated in the Anglo-American and Western European communities. It is basic to our democracy, for it presumes a society in which honest inquiry will lead to debate, by means of which questions of fact and policy will be decided ultimately by decision of the majority. Truth and justice will triumph—if they are adequately championed. But minds "warped by emotion" will accept whatever probability is made to appear most appealing to them. Abraham Lincoln was troubled (as have been many before and after him) by the fact that rhetoric can often lead to erroneous or harmful conclusions, and he phrased an aphorism which has become famous as a warning against unethical persuasion: " You can fool all the people some of the time, and some of the people all the time, but you can't fool all the people all the time." Cynics may observe that even if Lincoln was right, the odds remain heavily loaded in favor of error.

Well mindful of its limitations and dangers, Aristotle identified four uses of rhetoric: (1) to maintain truth and justice; (2) to deal with popular audiences (whose information or expertness is not particularly specialized in regard to the topic) ; (3) to provide a means of determining and displaying the various aspects of a controversial question; and (4) to defend ourselves against attack. The first use links rhetoric to logic, dialectic, and the scientific method. The third and fourth are practical arms of ethics. And the second is the core of his rhetorical theorizing.

The chief weakness of Aristotelian rhetoric, as we evaluate its usefulness in the global diversity, is that it is designed to deal with a particular kind of man, rather than with mankind in general. Aristotle knew only a very restricted portion of the world, and his concern was particularly with the situation he confronted in Athens. With great skill he analyzed the motivational patterns of the individuals and the society that were available to his inspection. He felt no particular need to try to distinguish between human qualities that are *innate* and those that are *in-bred*. For a great many centuries after Aristotle, philosophers and rhetoricians were content to rest on the proposition that all human beings are essentially alike. It remained for the social scientists of very recent time to stress that "personality is a factor of the situation as well as of the person." Only within the past generation or two have we understood the immense influence of *acculturation*. Now we know that every individual is shaped and patterned by his traditions and culture. We know that every society places its imprint deep within the nature and habit-structure of each of its members. We know that within a given society the members can only say meaningfully to one another that which they all already basically believe. We know that the very manner of our perceiving and thinking is deeply affected by our language, customs, history, and accepted system of values. Aristotle's rhetoric was designed for Athens. It has proved valuable for the Western civilization which evolved significantly from this particular fountainhead of culture. So far as we have tested it in trying to apply it in dealing with other cultures that in basic ways are critically different from our own, the results have been frustrating and disappointing.

One further point is worthy of emphasis in this summation of our own patterns of thought. As we have previously indicated in Chapter VII, Western civilization evolved according to the Greek value system. Christianity enforced the teaching of the Athenians that primary value inheres in the integrity of the individual. In the eighteenth century, John Locke developed a philosophy of human equality, which led to the establishment of political democracy. Within this societal pattern, individuals are conceived to have freedom of will and equality of consideration. Every member of society has a voice that must be heard; a vote that must be counted. Questions of policy are definitely in the realm of probability, and the most persuasive appeals are those that win the votes which finally designate what is true—or at least sufficiently true to become the basis for united action. In this way Lockian politics have greatly re-enforced and substantiated the validity of Aristotelian rhetoric.

It has been validated, that is to say, for us—for our social and political ideas. It works within the situation shaped by our culture. Does it work across the boundaries of other cultures? Specifically, now, does it work as we deal with the Confucian value system?

As we compare Aristotelian and Confucian rhetoric, significant differences emerge. In the first place, Confucius was unconcerned with problems of dealing with a lay or popular audience. Many Western observers have agreed with the point of view expressed by Charles H. Parker, in his *Dog Eats Moon* (1950), when he says: "The Chinese are pre-eminently one of the reasoning peoples of the world. They like to think, and because they like to think, they like to talk. . . . The Chinese like to discuss things; they like to put their ideas down in the form of Confucian dialogues." However true this might be potentially for the whole population, historically only a tiny fraction of the people of China have been educated even to the point of literacy. With their hierarchal system, it has been sufficient to have the decisions pondered and made by small groups of leaders. And it was precisely this group Confucius had in mind as he considered how ideas should be formulated and influence exerted. His concern was for scholars highly trained in a common background of learning.

Because of this, the rhetorical method he implied was an art of persuasion primarily aimed at achieving agreement on abstract definitions of philosophical terms. Thus it has been concerned primarily with the first of Aristotle's four purposes: to maintain truth and justice. The emphasis has been upon what Aristotelian rhetoric terms *inventio*—the exploration of the nature of ideas, the validity of proofs, the significance of the topic. The central question dealt with has been, what should a man believe? From the great body of possible truth, how can we find a centrality of meaning? What elements of this truth can we utilize to affect conduct? What are the problems which can and must be dealt with?

In conformance with these two characteristics, of dealing with a learned audience on matters of essential truth, the Confucian method has abjured appeals to emotion and has stressed fact and logic. Its concern has been with what Plato in the *Phaedrus* called *psychagogy:* "the turning of men's souls toward truth."

As the centuries have passed, Confucian ideas have filtered down through the masses and, in doing so, have become both solidified and somewhat degraded. The inquiry to determine new truth largely gave way to delight in search for precedents by which to enshrine old truths. The concern with abstract principles, combined with the love of dispute, led to a high emphasis upon adjudication of differences. As Parker indicates in his entertaining and incisive *Dog Eats Moon,* when two Chinese get into an argument (as they often do) the entire village gathers around to enjoy the fun. The argument develops at great length and with great intricacy. Every possible element of significance is examined and re-examined. However strong the feelings may be, the desire to win a favorable decision is no more urgent than the sheer enjoyment of the thrust and parry of interminable debate. In this way there developed in China the fourth purpose of rhetoric which Aristotle envisaged: its use for attack and defence. The Jesuit priest, P. J. B. Du Halde, whose two-volume work, *A Description of the Empire of China and the Chinese,* was translated and published in London in 1738-41, noted with astonishment that, "In some Districts the People are so very litigious, that they mortgage their Lands, Houses, and Goods, and all that they have, for the Pleasure of going to Law."

These, then, are the chief characteristics of Confucian rhetorical thought, that are evident still today, even through the rough and heavy overlay of Chinese Communism: a dogmatic concern with abstract and final truth, rather than attentiveness to the particulars of the immediate situation; a belief that decision-making is primarily to be confined to the elite; and a strongly argumentative turn of mind. Within this broad stream, however, various subdivisions have emerged through the course of the centuries. To a degree they color and influence one another; together they have made of Confucianism something vastly different from the original teachings of Confucius.

Out of the code of *Li,* or the five-fold relationships of individuals which Confucius devised as a major factor in his teaching, there developed the School of Li. The emphasis of this school, or sect, was upon the specific ceremonies through which these relations were to be conducted. Its proponents invented and thence safeguarded an extremely elaborate code of behavior which prescribed explicit forms of conduct for all foreseeable types of human relations. Because the prescribed rituals were easily to be seen, they lent themselves readily to policing and took on great importance in Confucian society. The School of Li was charged with the conduct of the annual examinations by which officials were selected for governmental positions, so that for centuries it remained the dominant school of Confucianism.

Du Halde himself noted "above three thousand" prescribed modes of behavior, and was interested to observe that they were as rigidly enforced in the rural areas as in the cities—among the poor and illiterate as well as among the cultured classes. In view of the intricacy of the rituals as well as their multiplicity, he noted wryly that "It is a difficult Matter for a Stranger to conform himself to their Notion of Politeness and Civility." Nevertheless, his conclusion was that "It is a Task to learn them and a Science to be a Master of them; but they are brought up to them from Infancy, so that, however irksome they may prove at first, they at length become natural to them."

Douglas C. Haring encountered this same Confucian ceremonialism in Japan, after World War II, and found it had great social utility, although he regretted that the cost was the submersion of individuality. "Even within the family," he noted in a chapter he wrote for Ralph Linton's *Most of the World* (1949), "etiquette restrains expression. Children approach their parents with bows and formal phrases. Husband and wife avoid public display of affection. In the service of etiquette the language has attained esoteric complexity, with separate vocabularies for the sexes, for differing degrees of social status, and for formal occasions; elaborate circumlocutions protect the polite fictions of 'face'."

How this ritualism works in practice is that it settles most problems before they arise. When two strangers in America approach a public water fountain simultaneously, there is no agreed upon formula for determining which one will drink first. In Confucian societies, if there is a difference in sex, age, or obvious social status, the inferior decisively steps aside and leaves the fountain for the superior. If the two seem at first glance to be of equal status, one will quickly ask the other to drink first; the second will refuse; the first will then touch his lips to the water and step back; the second will then drink, to be followed by the first. There is no doubt in the minds of either as to how to proceed. It is all done according to the dictates of *Li*.

During the Age of Sung (960-1279 A. D.), and under the influence of the great scholar Chu Hsi, the concern of Confucianism was largely with this matter of social doctrine or ritualistic behavior. Gradually there developed a philosophical justification that was independent of simple authority. Behind all the sensory appearances of nature, the School of Li taught, there lies a Supreme Ultimate, what Aristotle called the "first cause," which comprises the basic moral law of the universe. This law expresses itself through five elements: (1) benevolence, which partakes of the nature of wood and spring; (2) righteousness, which resembles metal and summer; (3) propriety, which is akin to fire and autumn; (4) wisdom, which has attributes of fire and winter; and (5) dedication, or loyalty, which reflects all nature.

As this philosophical trend developed, the School of Li merged into the School of Moral Law. It taught that man's first requirement is to achieve virtue by practicing self-control, and that he can do this only as he increases his knowledge. The idea is similar to the Platonic notion that to know is to be (or do) good. The question of what is to be known was answered: "That which has been known by the Sages." In other words, reflection would lead the individual thinker not to new and original conclusions but to conformity with the truths revealed in the classics.

In practice, the School of Moral Law discouraged practicality, concern with contemporary problems, and individuality. Its tenets were subordination of the mind and spirit to official doctrine and centralized rule. There is no doubt that these deeply-imbedded precepts, still influential in China today, help to account for the successful domination exercised by the Chinese Communists. Although commencing with an emphasis upon individual virtue, the chain of reasoning leads straight toward totalitarianism.

The philosophy of the School of Moral Law did not discourage analysis, but it turned the analytic inquiry away from concrete problems or situations and toward abstract terms. The proper topics of investigation were defined as the "Four-Seven Thesis"— which dealt not with the facts of nature but with the origin and characteristics of human motivation. In a rough paraphrase, the idea was not to subdue facts and divert them to human use, but to reshape thought and conduct in order to make them conform to the official interpretation of the facts. Here, then, lies the genesis of the Chinese Reds' invention of "brain-washing."

The four principles from which right conduct were thought to arise were identified as: charity, duty to neighbors, propriety, and wisdom. Opposing these principles of right conduct were the seven passions: joy, anger, sorrow, fear, love, hatred, and desire.

In Korea, which in the fifteenth and sixteenth centuries became the center of Confucian learning, there developed a split in the School of Moral Law, which led to its further sub-division. A scholar named Yulgok (1536-1584) was a monist, who insisted that the principles tending toward right conduct and the passions tending toward error are only differing manifestations of the same invariant force. He developed a rhetorical theory that sanctioned appeals to any or all of the seven passions as means of leading the listeners to live in accord with the four principles. Thus his rhetoric resembled that of Aristotle, who regretted that men are emotional, but felt that since they are, we must adapt our persuasive means accordingly.

Opposing these ideas of Yulgok were three dualistic scholars, Hwadam (1489-1546), T'oege (1501-1570), and Kobong (1527-1572). They argued that nature and moral law are different; that nature is resistant to the antagonistic pressures of morality. In their view, the seven passions were derivative from nature, and the four principles were exemplifications of the moral law. The only proper mode of argumentation, as they conceived it, is to lead the auditor away from so much as awareness of the existence in himself of the seven passions. Yulgok was a student not only of Confucius but also of Buddha, and his monism surely derived in large part from the Hindu and Buddhist *sutra,* or scriptures.

In our view the entire controversy may seem unreal, for it was carefully safeguarded from the contamination of contact with the everyday realities of practical problems. Abstraction was the only plane on which argumentation could properly be conducted. Nevertheless, the School of Moral Law's theorizing involved inquiry into the essential nature of man and the means by which human nature may with propriety be influenced. It was a rhetoric that for centuries had a decisive influence on the modes of thinking of the scholastic and political community of Confucianism. It would be foolhardy to believe that it does not still exercise influence today.

The School of Rites arose in the late sixteenth century as a reversion against the abstract theorizing of the School of Moral Law. It was, in fact, a conservative reaction toward the doctrines of the earlier School of Li. The teaching of this school was the rigid adherence to a highly formalized set of rites or ceremonial patterns of behavior. Accordingly, it was less concerned with what Aristotle called *inventio,* the discovery, investigation, and evaluation of ideas, than with *memoria* and *pronunciatio,* or *elecutio*—or the modes by which communication is conducted. Not what is said, but how, was the concern of the School of Rites. Their appeal was back to Chu Hsi, in the germinal period of Confucianism, and their Sage was the Korean scholar, Kim Chang-saeng (1548-1631). His most influential disciples were his son, Kim Chip (1574-1656), Pak Se-Ch'ae (1631-1695), and Song Chung-gil (1606-1672).

The teachings of the School of Rites dealt with precedent, protocol, ritual, ceremony—with precise rules governing costume, language, music, art, and such activities as eating, drinking, working, fighting, and conducting disputations. Whether the immediate concern was trying a case in court or conducting foreign policy, whether settling a dispute over the use of an irrigation ditch or deciding on the education of children, the important consideration was less the facts of the matter than the proper mode of procedure.

Within the family, since Confucius had once observed that one should be silent while eating (perhaps because at the moment he was weary of talk), for centuries meals in Confucian homes have been eaten in silence. Children's relations with their parents, and the husband's with his wife, are governed by strict ceremonialism. In public life, the policies a man advocates or the depth of his understanding of issues were of less importance than whether he comported himself with propriety and in accordance with custom. Arguments flourished over what was the right decorum to be observed in new or ill-defined situations. In all matters of thought and behavior, form was of far more importance than matter. On such questions factions arose and energy was dissipated. Even today the five rules of the Confucian *Li* are of far more than passing importance.

These five rules, as we have noted, govern all the relations of subject to ruler, of wife to husband, of children to parents, of youth to their elders, and of neighbor to neighbor, or friend to friend. A son, for example, does not smoke in the presence of his father. A wife walks a dutiful three steps behind her husband. It is polite to inquire the age of a stranger if he appears to be older than the inquirer; but if a mistake is made and the responder actually is the younger of the two, the one who asks the question quickly conceals the fact by murmuring, "My elder one," with a bow of submissiveness. We may feel that such elaboration of ritual is artificial. But in effect it established a dependable code of acceptable conduct, thereby eliminating a vast number of disagreements, preventing hurt feelings, and providing a medium through which differences of opinion may be resolved with equal satisfaction to both parties.

The Wang School of Confucianism was founded by a Chinese scholar, Wang Yang-ming (1472-1528), who, like Yulgok, was a monist. Wang was influenced by Taoism, from which he derived a high regard for individualism. He took direct issue with the Chu Hsi, or orthodox, view that understanding can only be achieved through a study of the classics.

On the contrary, Wang believed that nature and nature's laws are one and indissoluble. This being so, man is necessarily a part of the oneness of nature. Being a part of the whole, an individual can gain access to truth through personal experience, which gives rise to insight. Like the Taoists, then, and in opposition to Confucius, Wang distrusted rational thought and emphasized the roles of sympathy and empathy. The problem of an individual, he believed, is so to discipline himself that he will be attentive solely to relevancies, avoiding all distractions. This view led him to practice and advocate an austerity of life that is somewhat akin to the rigors of present-day Zen Buddhism.

Believing as he did in the power of individual insight, Wang had little interest in either the elaborate ceremonialism of the School of Rites or the examination of the four principles and the seven passions which intrigued the attention of the School of Moral Law. His emphasis upon individualism was antithetical to the hierarchal system of subordination which was so useful to the Court and proved of special appeal to the farmers and merchants in the country districts. This fact, in turn, still further strengthened the tendencies of the school to ignore scholasticism (if only because libraries were not at hand) and to depend more and more upon analysis of individual experience.

Forced to operate in the provinces, this rhetorical tradition became more concerned with practical problems, with analysis of facts, and with persuasion through appeal to the emotions. Thus it developed more closely than did the other schools in accord with the Aristotelian tradition. Since facts are facts, who-ever may note them, and since concern with practical problems tends to elevate the status of who-ever can solve them, the School of Wang also encouraged the idea of egalitarianism. Undoubtedly it exercised influence in the development of the extensive systems of village democracy in China and in Korea (to which latter country it was introduced by Hagok (1647-1736), leader of a faction that lost favor and was exiled from Court.

Through its very nature, the Wang School left comparatively little literature to explain or justify its views. Essentially it was an Oriental prototype of the Peasants Revolt, which broke out in England in 1381 under the leadership of Wat Tyler and John Ball. Its philosophical effects, however, may still be discerned in the sturdy independence and common sense practicality of the Orient's rice paddy farmers.

Somewhat akin to the practicality of the School of Wang was the Legalist School, which developed in the fifteenth century. This school managed to flourish at Court and in the major cities, for it turned its attention to solving problems of government. The most notable break with the past advocated by the Legalists was in their concern with reforming administration rather than defending the privileges of the aristocratic class.

The central doctrine of the Legalist School was the need to clarify and codify the operations of the law, to reduce the effects of favoritism and inefficiency. This school turned in distaste from the abstractions of terminological disputation, and sought to spell out regulations that would operate realistically in dealing with practical problems. New codes of punishment and penalties were promulgated and new rules of conduct were adopted—not in terms of ancient ritual but in conformity with the observed conditions of everyday life.

With a view to reduce the evils of centralization of government and absentee landlordism, the founders of the Legalist School revised the five-fold Confucian *Li* into a "village contract." This code came to have the effect of common law, with its provisions enforced by local scholars. Numerous guilds were also established, to provide on a cooperative basis for the expenses of weddings and funerals, the borrowing of money, the harvesting of crops, the sale of the harvest, and the enforcement of local laws. Moreover, there was inaugurated a system of secret inspection by agents from the Court, to assure the just operation of local government. In furtherance of this new emphasis upon localism, Confucian schools and shrines were established in many localities.

The rhetorical influence of the Legalist School lay in its appeal from centralized autocracy and from the traditionalism of a dead past to defined codes of current law that met immediate and practical conditions. Not classical scholarship but the problems of the day became the concern of its followers.

A Korean derivative of the Legalist School (which, in turn, exercised much influence in China and Japan) was the Sirhok School, founded by the great scholar Pange (1622-1673). Pange became greatly concerned with the fact that the great Ming dynasty in China had been overthrown by the much smaller Manchu faction. He was also troubled by the tragedies accompanying the invasion of Korea by the Japanese warlord Hideyoshi, in 1592-98, and again by the Manchus in 1627 and in 1636-37. Something, he felt, must be amiss with the mode of government; and he tried to discover what.

The weaknesses that rendered both China and Korea indefensible, he felt, arose from their factionalism, rigidity of class distinctions, ultranationalism, isolationism, traditionalism, ritualism, and lack of concern for pressing economic and social problems. In other words, the abstraction and traditionalism of the old rhetorics had not provided suitable means for maintaining the welfare of the realm. The very process he engaged in, of seeking to determine what was wrong by examining the facts (rather than reference to classical scholarship) constituted a new spirit in rhetoric.

As one fruit of this new influence, a follower of Pange, Chong

Yak-yong (1762-1836) wrote a long and scholarly criticism of the Confucian classics, pointing out weaknesses and shortcomings in the treatises on economics, politics, medicine, phonetics, geography, and poetry. He fought for administrative reforms within the government until he fell into disfavor and was exiled; and even then his example led to the establishment of the cabinet system of advisers to the Emperor, whereby policies were determined by discussion and argument.

Through the Wang, the Legalist, and the Sirhok Schools, a new spirit of practical realism was injected into the ancient forms of Confucianism. Today both the old forms and the new spirit remain, both aspects exercising strong influence on the thought and behavior of the hundreds of millions of convinced Confucianists.

Chapter 10

RHETORICAL IMPLICATIONS IN TAOISM

Taoism is without doubt the most confused and confusing of the major world idea-systems. Its origin stems from that same Fifth Century B. C. that gave rise to Confucianism and Buddhism. Like these other two, it has held an enormous following. In many respects the three great Oriental religiophilosophies have become so intertwined as to be inseparable. Each is hospitable to the others, and in many families various members identify themselves with two or all three of them. Nevertheless, each has its own distinct imprint—its own special influence in shaping personality and manner of thought. But Taoism is the most difficult of analysis.

The essence of Taoism is irrationality. This factor has made it especially appealing to Existentialists, and especially congenial to psychiatry. In the Far East, for many centuries, the wholesome aspects of Taoism were submerged—the great body of Taoist believers being illiterate country people who interpreted it as a mass of superstitions that penetrated into every aspect of their lives. Then the Taoist philosophy entered into the formation of Zen Buddhism, and became again a subject for serious study.

The Taoist way of looking at meaning differs more from the traditional Western rationalism than does either Confucianism or Buddhism. Hence, it is when we encounter Taoist modes of thought or behavior in our dealings with the Orient that we feel most tempted to agree with Bret Harte that "The heathen Chinee is peculiar." So skilled an interpreter of the East to the West as Lin Yutang has declared that the great Taoist classic, the *Tao-Teh-Ching,* is the "one book in the whole of Oriental literature which one should read above all others." Its very difference is a source of its value—this plus its long and wide popularity.

The *Tao-Teh-Ching* is the briefest of all the great world scriptures. It is comprised of eighty-one poems, written in 5,000 Chinese characters. Parts of it are as clear as the Sermon on the Mount, parts as obscure as portions of the Book of Revelations. The insistency of its appeal to Western as well as Oriental readers is indicated by the fact that it has been translated oftener than any other book except the Bible—more than a dozen times into English, for example, and nine times into German. It has also been the least understood of the great religious classics—a point readily underscored by the wide diversity of explanations of its ambiguities and paradoxes. However, despite the vast amount of scholarship devoted to its analysis, never to this date has anyone attempted to derive from its ideational system its rhetorical implications. Perhaps as we view it from this point of view, we may be able to ascertain some of the ways in which the Oriental mind sees reality and relationships differently than do we who have been nurtured on the Aristotelian rhetoric.

Difficult is its understanding may be, the reward is also uncommon. For one thing, Taoism (along with Zen Buddhism), after centuries of quiescence, is experiencing a resurgence of interest and influence. Something within it—perhaps chiefly its basic irrationality—makes it peculiarly attractive to our own age. It is one form of ancient wisdom that offers a key to doors of understanding that have remained closed to other modes of inquiry. As we search for "all available means" of unlocking the sealed vaults of human motivation, the "Way" of Taoism should not be overlooked. It is one way of penetrating into the mind-set of the imperturbable East.

Superficially, Taoism is essentially anti-rhetorical. "In much talk there is great weariness. It is best to keep silent." This is the theme of the fifth of the 81 poems that comprise the *Tao-Teh-Ching*. "Root out your preachers, discard your teachers, and the people will benefit a hundred-fold," reads part of the unusually rich 19th verse. "To be always talking is against nature," Lao-Tzu says in verse 23, for (as verse 22 asserts) "quietness is lord and master of activity." According to verse 2, "Wise is the man who teaches by deeds, not by words," and in verse 43 we are told that "The best instruction is not in words." Moreover, says verse 72, "The wise man knows himself but does not reveal his inmost thoughts." Since, according to verse 81, "True words may not sound fine and fine words may not be true," verse 73 warns, "It is not in words that God gets answers." For such reasons, verse 43 declares that "the greatest eloquence is like stuttering," and verse 81 advises that "A good man does not argue." Justifying his pacifism, in verse 43 Lao-Tzu avers that "If you do not quarrel, no one on earth will be able to quarrel with you." In verse 81 he notes gallantly that "The female always overcomes the male by her stillness."

Will Durant, in his compendious *Our Oriental Heritage* (1935), accepting the apparently anti-rhetorical implications of Taoism, offers this summation of Lao-Tzu's philosophy:

> Knowledge is not virtue; on the contrary, rascals have increased since education spread. Knowledge is not wisdom, for nothing is so far from a sage as an 'intellectual.' The worst conceivable government would be by philosophers; they botch every natural process with theory; their ability to make speeches and multiply ideas is precisely the sign of their incapacity for action.

Still further supporting this anti-rhetorical interpretation is the passage in verse 81 of the *Tao-Teh-Ching* which reads in part: "Those who are skilled do not dispute; the disputatious are not skilled. . . . The Sage constantly keeps the people without knowledge and without desire; and where there are those who have knowledge, he prevents them from presuming to act. . . . He who tries to govern a state by his wisdom is a scourge to it, while he who does not do so is a blessing."

Comparing these views with our Western heritage, it is interesting to note that Plato, who, in *The Republic*, defended the idea that the best government is that by a philosopher-king, in his late work, *The Laws*, abandoned that idea and concluded that the isolated wisdom of individuals is not adequate to solve the problems of a whole people. Recent presidential administrations in the United States have depended heavily on the guidance of "brains trusts" and professors-without-portfolio, with what effects each voter must decide for himself. In any event, they have brought government a long way from the Taoist-like view of Thomas Jefferson that "That government is best which governs least." Concurrently, psychologists are accumulating evidence that specialized education and high intelligence are no barrier to rationalization; on the contrary, they assist in making it more intricate and believable. This, no doubt, was the basis for Lao-Tzu's conclusion that "He who tries to govern a state by his wisdom is a scourge to it." The suspicion of intellectualism may be one reason why the intricate and detailed reasoning compact in many of the Western speeches at the United Nations does not receive a very sympathetic hearing.

If we dropped our examination of Taoism at this point, it would appear that, far from being a guide to rhetorical effectiveness, its chief lesson seems to be to avoid knowledge, to abjure facts, to abandon reason, and to remain silent. But, left at this point, analysis has not proceeded far enough. Taoism does, in fact, suggest a special mode for influencing human thought and conduct—but it differs significantly from the ways our culture has taught us to take for granted.

An accepted translation for the title of Lao-Tzu's book is "The Canon of the Way and of Virtue." Its principal teaching, as interpreted by H. G. Creel, the University of Chicago Sinologist, in his *Chinese Thought from Confucius to Mao Tse-tung* (1960), is that we "should be in harmony with, not in rebellion against, the fundamental laws of the universe." Despite what he said about teaching, Lao-Tzu himself was a teacher—as were his chief disciples, Chuang-Tzu and Yang Chu. By precept and example, these moulders of Taoism taught a way of life, a system of conduct, an interpretation of personality, a manner of dealing with oneself and one's fellows. Since the influencing of men was their chosen mission, we cannot take seriously the disclaimer of Chuang-Tzu:

> *Tao* cannot be heard. Heard, it is not *Tao*. It cannot be seen.
> Seen, it is not *Tao*. It cannot be spoken. Spoken, it is not *Tao*.
> That which imparts form to forms is itself formless; therefore,
> *Tao* cannot have a name. What there was before the universe
> was *Tao*. *Tao* makes things what they are, but it is not itself a
> thing.

Unquestionably, "that which imparts form to forms" is rhetoric. It is, to borrow a phrase from Ralph Waldo Emerson, "the art of putting things." Taoism is a mode of interpreting facts and an explication of motivational factors; it is precisely for this reason that for a millenium it exercised enormous influence and is once

again coming into prominence. Far different from the rhetoric of
Aristotle, it merits examination not alone for whatever vision of
truth it may represent but also because (regardless of its validity)
it shaped and now is helping to reshape the nature of the communion and communication of millions of individuals in that
Orient with which we must somehow learn how to come to terms.

To Lin Yutang there is no question that the *Tao-Teh-Ching*
is a book of rhetoric; but his thumbnail interpretation of its rhetorical significance (which must have been extremely casual) is
misleading. He calls it "the first enunciated philosophy of camouflage in the world," and he declares, "it teaches the wisdom of appearing foolish, the success of appearing to fail, the strength of
weakness and the advantage of lying low, the benefit of yielding to
your adversary and the futility of contention for power." He adds
that "If one reads enough of this Book, one automatically acquires
the habits and ways of the Chinese." Whatever may be the merit of
his interpretation, the last sentence is indeed high tribute to the
rhetorical power of Taoism. Noting the profoundly ethical character of the work, Yutang quotes from verse 61: "The virtuous man
is for patching up, the vicious man for fixing guilt." This perhaps
is a sufficient rebuttal of his own summation of Lao-Tzu's rhetoric
as a "philosophy of camouflage."

Among the difficulties of interpreting the rhetoric of Lao-Tzu,
the first is the question of when and even of whether he ever lived.
Lin Yutang confidently notes his birthdate as "about 570 B.C.,"
and Will Durant also follows the traditional view that he was
"pre-Confucian." Actually, if Yutang's date is correct, Lao-Tzu
was almost an exact contemporary with both Confucius and Gautama Buddha. Creel, however, points out that the *Tao-Teh-Ching*
contains ideas that can only be refutations of later abuses of Confucianism. Noting also that the work contains contradictions and
differences of style, he believes that Lao-Tzu probably never
existed, that if he did his dates are some two centuries later than
formerly supposed, and that rather than being an individual
philosopher he was in effect (like Homer) a composite of preceding views.

The traditional view at any rate is that Lao-Tzu, past the age of eighty, weary of his work as Curator of the Royal Library, and disgusted with the knavery of the Court of Chou, sought to flee from the kingdom. The warden of the frontier guard, Yin Hsi, stopped him and insisted that before he could depart he must write down his wisdom as precepts for the people. Whatever may have been its origin, the *Tao-Teh-Ching* is a unique contribution to the understanding of the mysterious ways of human conduct.

The *Tao* is generally translated as "the Way." It is presented as *the way* to find one's true relation with eternal essence. The chief guide-posts along this way are "wu-wei" (avoidance of action), "wu-hsin" (negation of mind), and "te" (the principle of spontaneous functioning). In verse 4 of the *Tao-Teh-Ching* the Way is called " a preface to God," and in verse 9 the goal is identified as peace. As nearly as we can state it, the meaning of the Way seems to be that *to do* is nothing; *to be* is all. It seems akin to Jesus' pronounced preference for the way of Martha over that of Mary, Again to cite the Emersonian paraphrase: "Do not *say* things." For, "What you are stands over you and shouts so loud I cannot hear what you say."

The Taoist ideal of mentality would seem to be not serenity but passivity. Whatever there is to be gained must be gained without trying. In Taoism is to be found the explanation for the saying of Jesus which has proved so puzzling to our Western minds: "The meek shall inherit the earth." A clear statement of this theme it to be found in the Book of Chuang-Tzu, a fourth century B. C. disciple of Lao-Tzu, who wrote: "The perfect man employs his mind as a mirror. It grasps nothing; it refuses nothing. It receives, but does not keep." Lao-Tzu himself said, in verse 20, "Cut out cleverness and there are no anxieties." Instead, as he said in verse 19, "Cherish sincerity."

Just what, then, did Lao-Tzu and his followers conceive to be the solution for the tangled problems of living with oneself and with our fellows? Confucius, troubled by the inability of human beings to deal with the complexities of our own yearnings and the uncertainties of the socio-physical environment, advised that the best solution is to yield to the governance of a strict code of conventionality. In this wise, every man will know what to expect of himself and his fellows. The paths of duty and of social propriety will be clearly marked. In sharp contrast, as is stated in the 25th verse of the *Tao-Teh-Ching,* "The principal of Tao is spontaneity." The New England Transcendentalists, praising individualism as against conformity, were followers of the *Tao.*

So were they when they praised intuition and insight as against reason. To Lao-Tzu, truth is never to be discovered by analysis— but always and forever by empathic feeling. According to Chuang-Tzu, our personal and social problems arise primarily because "Men one and all value that part of knowledge which is known [or to be discovered]. They do not know how to avail themselves of the Unknown in order to reach knowledge. Is not this misguided?" Lao-Tzu similarly, in verse 19, advised: "Cut out sagacity; discard knowingness." In verse 21 he explains:

> The Tao is something blurred and indistinct.
> How blurred! How indistinct!
> Yet within it are images.
> How blurred! How indistinct!
> Yet within it are things.
> How dim! How confused!
> Yet within it is mental power.
> Because this power is most true,
> Within it there is confidence.

These principles of spontaneity and intuition are but elaborations of the guide-posts to the Way: "wu-wei" (receptivity), "wu-hsin" (mindlessness), and "te" (spontaneous functioning.) Like the scepticism of David Hume, they see the essence of "knowledge" as lying not in an objectified world of external reality but in the insight of the knower. Like Hans Vaihinger, they assume that we live in a world not of "as is" but of "is if"—but that the *interpretation* is the sole reality of which we can ever be aware. Like Walter Lippmann, these Taoist principles indicate that "For the most part [they would eliminate this timorous qualification] we do not first see, and then define, we define first and then see." Like Charles Keyser, they see significant utterances as being "doctrinal functions"—modes of interpretation—although they go further than he in assigning prime significance to the "functional" as against the "descriptive" character of the statements.

Taoism is most often cited as the opposite of Confucianism; and indeed the Tao is the negation of formalistic conventionality. However, Lao-Tzu did not interpret "unconventional" as the flouting of convention. In ancient China, as in our own contemporary world, the flat rejection of social values would have meant imprisonment, exile, excommunication, or death. This kind of flagrant negativism could never lead to "peace," the goal of the Way. What Lao-Tzu meant by "unconventionality" is akin to the lessons we learn from anthropology and social psychology, namely: to attain to an understanding of the relativity and expediency of social customs. It is this understanding which serves as a protective shield to preserve us from the deadening effects of conformity.

Be not deceived by conventional custom, Lao-Tzu pleaded. Understand that it is neither more nor less than a social agreement which has currency because of its transient convenience. See through appearances to the reality which is veiled by customary modes of interpretation. It was only when people lost sight of the way to live, according to Witter Bynner's interpretation of Taoism, that it proved necessary to invent such concepts as love, honor, charity, and the encaptivating mould we call "education." These codes being in opposition to reality, hypocrisy became the ruling social virtue—a motivational pattern originating in pretense, designed to misdirect the prying eyes of neighbors, and always in basic disharmony with nature.

If this interpretation is correct, Lin Yutang's ascription of "the philosophy of camouflage" to Lao-Tzu is fundamentally in error. It is true that Lao-Tzu advocated a sufficiency of "outward conformity" (and it must be to this that Yutang referred) ; but the emphasis of the *Tao-Teh-Ching* is upon piercing through the exterior shield to the inner truth.

Interpreted in this fashion, Taoism appears to have startling analogies with Freudian psycho-analysis. Despite the conflict between Self and Society, Lao-Tzu (like Freud) did not believe that peace is to be found through flouting social conventions. Neither would he countenance a hypocritical subservience to their dictates. There is a better way, he felt—a way of sufficient outward conformity to avoid rejection while being simultaneously true to one's own inner vision of truth.

The first requirement is to know what is true. This cannot be accomplished by reason or by analytical intelligence but by a non-mental, non-active insight. "He also sees who only stands and waits." Alan Watts, in *The Way of Zen* (1959), interprets the Taoist method as the utilization of "the peripheral vision of the mind." Like the Buddhists, the Taoists believed that "no mind is the true mind." Paradoxical as this may seem, our own psychology concurs—at least to an extent.

In many aspects of living, we do best that to which we give least thought. Speech itself is an excellent illustration; if we tried to govern consciously the complex of muscles and nerves with which we speak, we never could utter, for example, such a phrase as "the Methodist Episcopal Church." We breathe and walk, both very complex activities, without thinking of the processes. We ride a bicycle well only after we stop thinking about how to do it. In whatever activity we become most skilled, large and important portions of the act-complex become automatic. In other words, we attain to greater efficiency (even to greater mental efficiency) by withdrawing our minds from active supervision.

Similarly, we realize, too, that non-awareness is often the chief characteristic of contentment. As Chuang-tzu says: "To be unaware of one's feet implies that the shoes are easy." It is in this sense, according to the Taoists, that true peace comes from ceasing to strive, to criticize, to think. "Tao always does nothing and yet it achieves everything." In the remarkably modern words of Yang Chu, from the *Lieh Tzu*, a fourth century B. C. text of Taoism: "We waste ourselves in a mad scramble, seeking to snatch the hollow praise of an hour, scheming to contrive that somehow some remnant of reputation shall outlast our lives." Our own Western paraphrase is the aphorism, "Happy is the country that has no history."

We half-know also that we often learn most truly that which we do not study. When we walk into a strange room, we may consciously notice a few large objects, but our peripheral vision takes in a wide range of unnoted items; and it is from this totality that our impression of the room takes form. We see a play and may like or dislike it—yet when we try to explain the nature of and the reasons for our reaction, our words sound hollow, artificial, and contrived in our own ears. We *know* that our reaction derives from far more and from far other reasons than those which our critical faculties can represent.

Intelligence, to the Taoist, is not the analytic activity of the cortex. It is, rather, the totality of the "feeling tone" which eventuates from a vast complex of factors impossible to identify. The *Tao* is "blurred and indistinct . . . . . Yet within it are images." The way to see, to comprehend, these images is not to try to understand them, not to search for them, but to wait. The mind should be like a mirror, neither seeking nor rejecting—merely reflecting. Above all, thinking should not be purposive, for this means a sharpening of focus that shuts out or diminishes everything except the preconceived definition of the situation.

Analytic intelligence always misrepresents—never can possibly discover or define reality; for truth is an inner essence with such multiple manifestations that any one formulation of it must deny or ignore much of its meaning. Emerson well phrased this insight of the Taoists in his famous lyric which begins:

> If the red slayer thinks he slays
> Or if the slain think he is slain,
> They know not well the subtle ways
> I keep, and pass, and turn again.

To know, then, requires not the "use" of mind but the permissive functioning which can only occur without direction. This freeing of the mind to utilize its own resourcefulness is far different from not thinking at all; it consists not of purposive control but the disciplined abandonment of controls over the senses and the muscles in order that they may "vacuously" pursue their own apparently randomized but natural investigations of nature. Rather than a planned investigation of self or of the environment, it presumes and permits a spontaneous functioning of the totality of the receptive mechanisms, including memory.

What, now, has this to do with rhetoric?

In the first place, the *Tao* is not, after all, a rejection of rhetoric. Lao-Tzu not only understood that speech is one of the social necessities, but he required that it be "good." In verse 27 he declares that, "Just as a good runner leaves no tracks, so does a good speaker make no blunders." Even more pointedly he adds, "Perfect speech is like a jadeworker whose tool leaves no mark." In verse 8 he established the criterion that "A good speech is judged by its truthfulness." When he said (in verse 45) that "the greatest eloquence is like stuttering," he must have meant that what is needed is a new conception of eloquence that should make it fit the expectations of the listeners. He indicated the "end" of rhetoric (peace) when he said in verse 81 that "It is not good to settle a grievance, if the settlement leads to other grievances."

The motivational philosophy of Taoism clearly was based upon identification of the speaker with his listeners. This emerges from the whole scheme of the Taoist thought and is rendered explicit by Chuang-tzu:

> Concerning the right and the wrong, the 'thus' and the 'not thus,' if the right is indeed right, there is no point in arguing about the fact that it is different from the wrong; if the 'thus' is indeed 'thus,' why dispute about the way in which it is different from the 'not thus'? Regardless of whether the various arguments actually meet one another or not, let us harmonize them within the all-embracing universe, and let them run their course.

Much of the fault in our discourse, according to Taoism, derives from trying too hard. "He who raises himself on tiptoe cannot for long remain steady," we are told in verse 24 of the *Tao-Teh-Ching*. In verse 46 we read that "There is no greater misfortune than not to know when one has enough," and in verse 9 Lao-Tzu says:

> If you would not spill the wine,
> Do not fill the glass too full.
> If you wish your blade to hold its edge,
> Do not try to make it over-keen. . . .
> When you have done your work and established your fame,
>   withdraw!
> Such is the Way of Heaven.

In sum, Taoism has much to say concerning *inventio:* with the what and the how of gathering matter for speech. Secondly, it has a great deal to do with *dispositio*—with the selecting, the arranging, and the pointing of the matter assembled. Thirdly, it has a sharp bearing upon audience adaptation and the selection of motivational appeals. Fourthly, it carries strong implications for the manner of speaking, the *elocutio* and *pronunciatio*. Finally, it provides the base from which Lao-Tzu derived his own notion of the role of speech in human affairs.

When we deal with Taoist peoples, then—and the spirit of Tao penetrates deeply and spreads pervasively through much of the Far East, over-lapping and inter-penetrating other idea-systems in the whole vast area from India and Southeast Asia to China, Korea, and Japan—there are several important considerations we should have in mind as guiding principles.

Perhaps the most cogent is that, in the Taoist view, man is not really a rational being, nor is truth to be conceived in terms of reason and logic. When we seek to "prove" the verity of our point of view by citing facts and demonstrating their logical conclusions, we should not be surprised if our Taoist listeners remain unmoved. Many times they will be saying to themselves, as they listen to us, "Yes, the facts are as you say; and your logic is sound; but somehow, I don't know how or why, I *feel* it to be different than you say." We ourselves have a relevant saying, "A woman convinced against her will is of the same opinion still." We know, too, that in the course of an evening of talk we may be pushed into a corner by superior logic or disconcerted by confrontation with facts which undermine our own convictions; yet by the next morning we shall have comfortably slipped back into our old preconceptions. In other words, Taoist irrationality—a vivid sense that reality is something beyond or other than simple reason—is not, after all, very different from much of our practice, however widely it may differ from our theory. The real difference is that when we launch upon formal discourse or when we are confronted with an issue that must be talked out, we feel impelled to bring forth an arsenal of facts and to assume a logical posture. It may often be more effective with a Taoist audience to indicate that regardless of the facts and irrespective of the logic of the situation, we somehow feel that such-and-such is the case. This approach may be greeted with approving nods and a genuineness of fellow feeling. Surely the Taoists are not altogether wrong when they try to *empathize* rather than *rationalize* their way to sound conclusions. But, right or wrong, if this is the way they do it, then this is the mode by which we can best communicate with them.

Secondly, it is wise to remember that Taoists are naturally suspicious of what they regard as undue decisiveness. Many questions, in their view, can best be answered only with a meditative silence. Others should be turned aside with an ambiguous or irrelevant reply. What they believe, and perhaps with sound insight, is that the truth of a matter often lies on the periphery of the subject, rather than in its center. Our penchant for commencing a discussion by precisely defining our terms and proceeding through an orderly sequence of related arguments seems to the Taoists to be too narrowly purposive. As they believe, it is impossible to analyze a problem with clarity until after it is thoroughly understood. Therefore, to commence a discussion with clarity of development is to assert that the conclusion is apparent even before the examination of it has started. Our reply, of course, is that we have gone through the process of initial analysis and of making up our own minds before the discussion itself commences. In other words, it is our mental habit to try to understand a subject before we commence to talk about it. But this is not "the way" of Taoism. Taoists believe it is more fruitful to engage in truly group evaluation. That is, it is better to start talking in the midst of mental haze, with no certainties, no preconceptions, no definitiveness of meaning. Then, as the talk slowly unfolds, thought flows into the problem from various sources, uncabined by preconceptions. The best operation of the total organism (not merely of the mind) occurs when there is a lack of focus—when the discussants are passive rather than purposive in their approach to the topic. A Taoist prefers to think that he does not know where he is going until after he arrives; and he may even be happy to admit that when he gets there, he may not understand fully where he is. "I don't know" is a phrase far easier for a Taoist to utter than it is for us. What we must remember is that this phrase doesn't imply, "I don't care." The Taoist cares as deeply as we do for truth; but he believes more than we do that truth is likely to emerge most surely when we wait for it, when we accept it as it comes, rather than when we set forth along a preconceived path in a predetermined manner to define a truth that accords with our own clear purposive design.

Thirdly, we will do well to recall that for a Taoist talking about an idea is often of less value than what we might call avoiding it. This, again, is a feeling that arises from the conviction that the whole truth involves a vast amount of peripheral meaning, much of which is too vague to be identified or even recognized consciously. The man of ready speech is a man who quickly imposes upon a set of facts his own interpretation. In the Western world, this value of mysterious silence is perhaps best recognized, at least among prominent leaders, by France's Charles de Gaulle. In De Gaulle's view of leadership, "There can be no prestige without mystery . . . in the designs, the demeanor and the mental operations of a leader, there must be always a 'something' which others cannot altogether fathom, which puzzles them, stirs them, and rivets their attention. Nothing more enhances authority than silence. It is the crowning glory of the strong, the refuge of the weak, the modesty of the proud, the pride of the humble, the prudence of the wise, and the sense of fools." Then he added: "To speak is to dilute one's thoughts, to give vent to one's ardor; in short, to dissipate one's strength; whereas, what action demands is concentration. Silence is a necessary preliminary to the ordering of one's thoughts." Taoists would agree.

As we turn, now, to an interpretation of Buddhist and Hindu rhetoric, we shall find similarities enough to re-inforce the value of learning to utilize these Taoist principles and differences enough to keep us alert to the demands of differing segments of the world audience.

Chapter 11

THE RHETORIC OF HINDU-BUDDHIST IDEA SYSTEMS

IN THE INTERNATIONAL community, India since 1948 has risen to a position of influence far in excess of its political, economic, or military power. The reason is sometimes ascribed to the mystical-practical voice of India, Jawaharlal Nehru. To some degree it is a residue of the tremendous reputation of Mohandas Gandhi. Inevitably this influence stems in part from the size of the Indian population and from the strategic location of the Indian sub-continent. Perhaps even more significantly the strength of India derives from its being the fountainhead of Hinduism and Buddhism—the twin faiths that dominate the conventions and traditions of that third of the human race who dwell upon, below and even in significant numbers above the Himalyan backbone of Asia.

Buddhism derived from Hinduism much as Christianity derived from Judaism, but by a natural evolution, without the trauma of a crucifixion to create ill-will. The teachings of these two faiths, which have so much in common, deeply affect the thinking of from eight hundred millions to a billion and more human beings. If we find the political course of India difficult sometimes to understand and even harder to accept, it is in large part because of our mental and emotional distance from the religio-philosophical patterns that for five thousand years have etched themselves deeply into the psyche of the people. Neutralism is a political artifact that has been sometimes helpful and more often harmful or at least distressing in the years since 1945. But it is no jerry-built contrivance hastily put together to meet the exigencies of the communist-democratic conflict. Quite the contrary, neutralism is an inevitable outgrowth of habits of feeling and thinking that have been implanted by the tutelage of more than one hundred fifty generations. A whole social structure and philosophical system support it. The Indians and their cohorts may be born with characteristics very much like those of babies in any other part of the world. But as they absorb the culture in which they are nurtured, their personalities and their minds take on the shapes and mannerisms, the substance and the symbols of their Buddhist heritage.

Modernism and nationalism are both late comers to Southeastern Asia and the Indian sub-continent. Nehru and many of his lieutenants exhibit the polish of Oxford and the *savoir faire* of Paris; but their minds and their manners, their emotions and their motives, are still reminiscent of the ancient Vedic hymns. As for the great masses of people whose destinies they direct, the sentiments and strictures of Hinduism and Buddhism are woven into the very fabric of their every-day thoughts. India remains, as Norman Cousins has well said, "a shared historical experience, an accumulation of anguished memories, a community of hopes . . . a wild assortment of centuries . . . the world's most prodigious bundle of paradoxes."

This is another of the major cultural prototypes with which somehow we of America and the West must learn to come to terms. Nehru has well stated what we must accept as a truism—no less urgent because it is obvious: "Today the sphere of even the individual has grown world-wide," he wrote in *The Discovery of India,* completed in 1946, on the verge of India's long-awaited independence, " and different concepts of social organization conflict with each other and behind them are different philosophies of life." This difference in the philosophies of peoples was and is much on the mind of Mr. Nehru. Again and again in this book, as elsewhere, he reverts to the theme, and in great detail he tries to clarify for the West the fact that India today is a derivative—and perhaps to some degree even a prisoner—of India past.

No one should under-estimate the vast and yeasty yearning of the mass of Indians and other East Asians to stretch forward into the beckoning age of productive technology. In one sense they are new pioneers, standing on the verge not of new lands but of new ideas and of excitingly new potentials. The goals they seek are decidedly of the future; the way they would pursue is decidely different from the way they and their ancestors have known. But to a significant degree this fact is a begging of the essential question. True, advancement is their aim and the future they envisage is one of hygiene and automation; but the mode of their think-

ing and their reacting is and must be the pattern built into their
society and their personality through centuries of slow accretion.
To reach toward the future is not to deny the past. The rhetoric
of Hinduism and Buddhism, like our own Aristotelian rhetoric, is
compact of the traditions of centuries. Indians think as they must
think, feel as they must feel—impelled by the weight of their own
traditions. To understand what it is that motivates them, we must
make far greater effort than we ever have to date. Knowledge becomes understanding and understanding emerges into familiarity
only over a long period of taking infinite pains. A feeling for
Buddhist rhetoric cannot be achieved by a determined effort of the
will. It has to be painfully and slowly fed into the blood stream.
Far too late and far too slowly we are beginning to make a start.
There is a long way yet to go.

The failure of understanding, of course, has not been all one-
sided. For centuries the highly cultivated Orient scorned the "barbaric" areas beyond its own borders and refused to seek any enlightenment not enshrined in its own classics. We of the West have
learned just enough of the East to consider it economically, politically, hygienically, and educationally inferior; while the East has
learned to dread the greater military and political power of the
West. Indian spokesmen at the United Nations are well-known
for their tendency to claim superior moral insight and purer
spirituality for their views, while deriding the materialistic selfishness of Western policies. In turn, Occidental comment on Oriental
policies is likely to be condemnation of their apparent lack of realism. Contacts between the two hemispheres have multiplied, but
understanding does not seem greatly aided by simple contiguity.
Meanwhile, there is urgent wisdom in the plea of Alan Watts that
"It is both dangerous and absurd for our world to be a group of
communions mutually excommunicate."

In few areas is mutual understanding more needed than in the
realm of rhetoric—that branch of philosophy which, as we have
pointed out, is devoted to the triad of relationships among subject
matter (or truth), speaker (or purpose), and listener (or action).
If this greater understanding is to be achieved, it must be through
exploration of the differing modes of thought which, within differ-

ing cultural norms, prescribe varied means of exerting influence through discourse to the end that facts as stated will affect conduct in accordance with culturally accepted moral principles. This is a complex way of saying with some precision what a well-known proverb puts with crude directness: "One man's meat is another man's poison." If we are to talk to the Buddhist portion of the world's population, we must become able to think with their thoughts and to feel as they feel. This does not mean that we should abandon ourselves in order to go to them. There remains solid truth in the observation of Ralph Waldo Emerson (himself an earnest student of Orientalism) : "Insist on yourself; never imitate. Your own gift you can present every moment with the cumulative force of a whole life's cultivation; but of the adopted talent of another you have only an extemporaneous half possession." To study Buddhism is not necessarily to become Buddhist. But we can only give of our own gift as we know what is needed and how it will be received. Moreover, there is much for us to take, if we but learn what to look for and how to discriminate.

Somewhere between the indifference we have manifested in the past and an unqualified spirit of indiscriminate enthusiasm there is a middle way of mature evaluation. This should be the mood we seek as we examine Oriental philosophy in a search for its rhetorical principles. Of course we cannot hope to leap headlong into mastery of its complexities. Our educational system needs to be recast to introduce the study of Buddha, Lao-tzu, and Confucius, along with Plato, Aristotle, and Locke. The difficulty of the project must not discourage our determination to proceed as far and as well as we can.

If we were steeped in the religio-philosophical tradition of Buddhism—as are one third of the world's population—what emphasis would we give to the desirability of trying to influence the behavior of others? Toward what ends would we try to shape their conduct—and our own? What means of persuasion would be, in Aristotle's term, "available" within the context of deeply-held Buddhist beliefs? What would be our conception of the innate nature of man, to which our persuasion would have to be adapted?

What, in short, are the rhetorical criteria we must comprehend

if we are successfully to analyze and evaluate the rhetorical implications of Buddhism? What rhetorical modes should we seek to
develop in order to influence, as now we must, the thought and
actions of hundreds of millions of a very diverse Buddhist populace? How can we analyze and shape our response to the persuasive impact which they seek to exert upon our policies? These
are the questions for which we must seek answers in the roots of
their tradition.

One difference between the East and the West in interests and
in motivation has long been insisted upon. This is the presumed
fact that the Occident has developed science and technology because we are realistic, we observe nature, and we have accustomed
ourselves to obeying nature's laws; in the Orient, on the other hand
(so it is asserted) the wise man is he who sits all day lost in a stupor
of self-hypnosis or perhaps seeking wisdom by meditating on the
irregular convexity of his own navel. So canny a historian as Will
Durant, for example, in his volume on *The Life of Greece*, explained the greatness of the Athenians by contrasting their science,
philosophy, literature, and art with the "autocracy, quietism, and
mysticism" of the Far East. All history (or, for that matter, all
writing or all thinking) is necessarily based upon selectivity of
data; and the teeming millions of Buddhists surely have produced
their own quota of autocrats, idle dreamers, and irrational mystics.
A good counter to this kind of evaluation of the Orient, however,
may be found in a book edited in 1942 by Arthur E. Christy, *The
Asian Legacy and American Life,* in which a bevy of experts spell
out many practical contributions in agriculture, medicine, social
and political science, ethics, art, and education which we of the
West owe to the Far East. Somehow the Orient has maintained a
huge population, for many centuries, in a relatively stable equili-
brium that has stressed personal contentment, viruous living, and
international peace. Much of the achievement rests squarely upon
irrationality (as we have seen in our view of Taoism) ; but all of it
depends on a hard-headed realism.

F. S. C. Northrop, indeed, whose *Meeting of East and West* has
stressed the practical effects of ideas, believes that the primary
distinction betweeen East and West is that the Orient bases its

thinking on immediate experience, whereas the Occident delights in philosophical generalizations.

As one clue to this difference, Northrop contrasts the ideographic symbols used in Chinese writing with the alphabetic languages of the West. In a Chinese composition, he points out, "each solitary, immediately experienced local particular tends to have its own symbol . . . . . Sentences, furthermore, in Chinese are constructed by setting such purely individual symbols the one after the other in columns in the order in which the items which they denote in immediate experience are associated." What is written down is what is thought-in-context at the moment of writing—just as happens with us also. Our grammar, however, imposes upon the words used a generalized pattern of meaning. To "read" Chinese, on the other hand, it is necessary to try to re-create the mood and circumstances of the writing. In my own experience in the Far East I have often noticed that when a group of scholars try to interpret the meaning of a Chinese text, they normally trace over the characters with their fingers then engage in a lengthy discussion amongst themselves, seeking to establish what it was that the author probably meant. From one point of view, this suggests an inexactness in Oriental writing; but it also might well mean that the meaning is far too exact to be readily transliterated into other words, at another time, under other circumstances.

In India, also, even down to the nineteenth century, writing was considered too imprecise a means of conveying meaning to have any great communicative importance. Until the seventeenth century, books were inscribed on leaves and sheets of bark, which were hung like washing on lines, and were called "treasure houses of the Goddess of Speech." What was truly meant was what was said at the time of composition. Then a rough approximation of this meaning was transmuted into visible symbols and "stored"; but what the true meaning might be could only be conjectured in terms of the personalities, the problems, and the intentions of the composers of the message. Reading became a search for precision— aided but also handicapped by the admittedly imprecise medium of written words.

In section 9 of Chapter V of *The Discovery of India,* Nehru considers this problem at length, concluding, "It is difficult to capture the meaning, much less the spirit, of an old word or phrase." As among the Chinese, so also in India, the reasoning is that the meaning which has been inscribed in print must be "talked into being" as groups of readers jointly try to interpret what the incomplete written symbols can only intimate concerning the complete meaning the writer had in mind. From such a background, it is easy to see why the "neutralist" Asians feel relatively little concern when a nation fails to abide by its written treaty commitments. Violation of promises can not truly be charged against them unless or until it becomes clear what promises they actually intended to make—something that cannot be determined by the words alone.

To Westerners, nurtured in our own literalistic traditions, this point of view seems maddeningly mystical and undependable. We have trained ourselves to believe that words do in fact mean what they say. Aristotle insisted that clarity is the first virtue of good style, and this view has consistently been upheld in our part of the world. What language means to the West is well illustrated in the poetic theory of William Wordsworth, as he explained it in 1789 in his *Preface to Lyrical Ballads*. He described poetry as "emotion recollected in tranquility," meaning that the intent of the writer is nurtured in remoteness from his immediate sensory experience, while he searches for a precise form of language that will say lastingly and dependably what he thought and felt. The test of good writing, in this view, is that it must mean the same thing for all readers, whatever the circumstances of the writing or the reading. It is true that in many books on language, we of the West remind ourselves that meaning cannot exist independently of its context. But we say this without really meaning it; whereas the Orientals mean it so thoroughly that they find little need to say it. They take it for granted that what is said today is meant in terms of today's conditions and may have to be re-interpreted tomorrow.

Interestingly enough, our own Western emphasis in research seems now to be trending toward a vision of truth and even toward modes of discovery that resemble curiously this intrinsic nature of Buddhist thought. The most notable evidence of this appears in the emerging interest in *heuristics* as a basic method of

research. Indeed, so influential a guide as Professor Polanyi insists
that the very essence of research has come to be considered as "the
heuristic act of leaping across a logical gap." Other scientific theorizers, like Alfred North Whitehead, for example, declare that
the scientific method is really a process of soaking oneself in factual
data while waiting for a flash of insight. In attempting to define
this process, our contemporary theorizers are reverting to much the
same point which was identified in ancient Buddhist philosophy:
the inarticulate or pre-linguistic process of mind. The vocabulary
the new research theorists use sounds Western, but the idea is
Buddhist. This is evident in the startling conclusion stated by
Polanyi: "If everywhere it is the inarticulate which has the last
word, unspoken and yet decisive, then a corresponding abridge-
ment of the status of spoken truth itself is inevitable." In other
words, we do not and can not "say what we mean." The words used
are but approximations, sometimes helpful, sometimes misleading.

As we have indicated earlier in this chapter, the final solution
will not be found by abandoning the largely successful practices
that have produced such productive results as are evidenced by
Western civilization. The contradiction between Oriental and Occidental processes of thinking is more a matter of emphasis than of
essence. Orientals stress the "unique particularity" of each separate
event; but, like us, they, too, find a genuine need for generalizations and for continuity of meaning. Like us, they recognize that
everyone brings to each fresh experience the memory and evaluative pattern evolved from his own past experience and from the
"social agglomerate" which has become an integral part of his own
personality through acculturation. Northrop quotes approvingly
the assertion of the Chinese Sage Tzu Ssu (a grandson of Confucius) that "entire realness never ceases for a moment." How,
then, are "entire realness" and "unique particularity" reconciled?

To Northrop the reconciliation consists in the Oriental view—
held in common by Taoists, Confucianists, and Buddhists—of a
"non-transitory, indeterminate aesthetic continuum." Whoever
would understand the thinking of the East must start by unrav-
elling the meaning of this "indeterminate aesthetic continuum."
It is indeterminate, for it evades precise definition or statement.

It is aesthetic, for real meaning deals with beauty, which is also truth, as fleeting manifested in particular forms. And it is all-embracing or continuous, uniting all individuals with the total environment, including the union of all individuals into one meta-physical being. Perhaps the most familiar Westernization of this concept is Ralph Waldo Emerson's Over-Soul. What it means is that no generalization or abstraction has significance except as it is materialized into some particular; but, concurrently, no single unit of experience can be meaningful except within its complete context, which is infinitely extensive, comprising all that is, was, or will be.

The greatest of the Indian poets, Kabir, confronted the question of how to deal with this endlessly extensive and timeless infinitude by advising that attention must be kept centered upon "unique particularity." "Put all imaginations away," he urged, "and stand fast in that which you are." Lin Yutang, who has devoted his life to interpreting the East to the West, dealt with this same problem in his 1942 volume, *The Wisdom of China and India,* where he said that the "ultimate reality" is in itself incomprehensible; but, since "the individual soul, or Self, within is identical with the soul without," no particular event or circumstance can be understood except by looking through and beyond it to its connection with the whole universe of being.

The primary rhetorical difficulty which confronts the Buddhists (and we who must deal with them) is this: that nothing can be said meaningfully except to depict accurately and in careful isolation an immediately experienced sensation; yet this depiction has no validity except as it is assumed to be indelibly united into the totality of all possible reality. It is a kind of problem that Aristotle, and we, his heirs, tried to avoid by positing, first, that every identifiable entity has a separatedness that makes it independently definable; and, second, that there are "general laws" of ethics, logic, and nature, according to which all unique objects and occurrences may be categorized.

Thus Aristotelian rhetoric assumes that (1) "this act is an act which can and must be evaluated according to analysis of what it inescapably is"; and (2) "this act is an act which must be evaluated in terms of its accord with or deviation from an established norm of ethics, expediency, or natural law." The Aristotelian method has never proved to be satisfactory, for it confronts us with a contradictory duality that constantly requires reconciliation. For this reason it is today under heavy attack both by scientific theorists and by the new logicians.

Buddhism quite differently solved its dilemma of reconciling "entire realness" with "unique particularity" by positing a monistic rather than a pluralistic universe. In this view, every particular act partakes inevitably of all the eternal verities. The problem for both speaker and listener is to discern the "aesthetic continuum" that lies within the finite act or object. The temptation, of course, is to define the infinite nature of the finite particular in terms pre-established by categorical, or dogmatic, or conventionalized systems. This temptation proved too strong for any except the greatest Sages to resist, leading to the formulation of so many divergent orthodoxies that Guatama Buddha found the Indians of the Sixth Century B. C. confused by sixty-three contending schools of philosophy. Long after the death of the Buddha, in our own times, the same dogmatizing tendencies continued and have in recent times been combatted by *Yoga*—"a method for finding out things for oneself rather than a preconceived metaphysical theory of reality or of the universe." In other words, Yoga in the midst of Buddhism is like Unitarianism in the midst of Christianity—a denial of creeds and an assertion of the need for individualized exploration of ideas.

Gautama Buddha, like Jesus, came to fulfill not to destroy the ancient wisdom. His interpretation of Buddhism derived directly from Hinduism. He turned in his meditation back to the Vedic Hymns, which date from as early as 4,000 B. C. In them God (Purusha) is represented as creating the world by destroying himself—that is, by dividing his indivisible being into apparent multiplicity. He created the universe, said Buddha, by "an act of self-dismemberment or self-forgetting, whereby the One became Many." In this sense, as Alan Watts playfully interprets it, "the world is God playing hide-and-seek with himself." Reality is a process of whirling parts seeking blindly to re-establish themselves as a whole. For, declared the Buddha, "This Purusha is all that yet hath been and all that is to be."

According to this hypothesis, wholeness or universality lies implicitly within every instance of particularity. Ugliness and evil are apparent only because they are incompletely interpreted. Inherent in every object and every act is beauty and goodness—the essential nature of God. It follows that "Any supposed truth which cannot be spoken in love and inward peace is not truth." Or, as Gautama Buddha phrased it, "The world does not know that we must all come to an end here; but those who know it, their quarrels cease at once."

Our concern is not with the life of Buddha, which is sketched in any good encyclopedia, nor with Buddhist philosophical doctrines, which are popularly explained in Alan Watts' *The Way of Zen,* Will Durant's, *Our Oriental Heritage,* and Joseph Gaer's *How the Great Religions Began,* but with the hitherto unexplored question of what rhetorical criteria derive naturally from the basic tenets of Buddhism. What we have established concerning the fundamentals of the Buddhist world view prepare us to seek Gautama Buddha's answers to the following four questions, which lie at the heart of rhetorical inquiry:

1. What is the purpose of inquiry? What is it that we seek to understand—and why?
2. What is the nature of truth? How do we judge in a given instance between truth and falsity?
3. What is the nature of man? What are the wellsprings of human motivation? By what means may men be led toward or diverted from truth?
4. On the bases of answers to the foregoing questions, what kind of discourse is effective? What are the responsibilities of speakers? What are the proper uses of speech?

Out of the teachings of the Buddha and the traditions of Buddhism, the following answers emerge.

1) The proper object of inquiry is to find the basic unity that lies within seeming diversity. When truth is properly comprehended, there is no cause for argument or dissent. For essential truth is comprehensive, incorporating within one indissoluble

whole all possible points of view, however divergent they may appear to be. This doctrine by itself is sufficient to explain Nehru's "neutralism" and seeming refusal to make moral judgments discriminating (for example) communism from democracy.

2) Truth, however, is not easily discerned; for general truth is apparently forever contradicted by particulars, each of which, judged in and by itself, is always a denial of truth. Hence, the contradiction between essential truth and its apparent contraries demands constant and exhaustive efforts at elucidation. This belief helps to explain the length and frequency of the speeches by Pandit Nehru and by his representatives at the United Nations. They are simply adhering to a long and deeply established Indian cultural trait. "Talk it out" would appear to be one of the social imperatives for those who have been nurtured on Buddhism.

This extreme talkativeness (which often is assertive and dogmatic) appears to violate the Buddhist renunciation of argumentation. Ideally, Buddhism declares, our thoughts should center upon universality, commonality, and (thus) the treatment even of enemies with love. In the most basic collection of sermons by Gautama Buddha, the *Dhammapada,* Chapter XVII develops the theme: "Let a man overcome anger by love, let him overcome evil by good; let him overcome the greedy by liberality, the liar by truth." But, as will appear when we examine the next of our questions, ideal methods cannot be utilized in this imperfect universe. Monistic unity has been dissevered into multiplicity; understanding is prevented by the prevalence of error. Therefore, as the Buddha admonished in Chapter V of the *Dhammapada,* as a wise man does see the truth, "Let him admonish, let him teach, let him forbid what is improper! He will be beloved by the good; by the bad he will be hated." It is clear from Buddha's own practice that he believed in the active conversion of unbelievers. When sharpness seemed to be necessary, he himself was harsh. These methods of propagating truth, however, were merely expedient. In the concluding chapter of his sermon collection, Gautama phrased what surely he most deeply felt: "Him I call indeed Enlightened who utters true speech, instructive and free from harshness, so that he offends no one." Thus far it appears that Buddhism, holding a vision of all-encompassing truth, encourages exposition rather than argument, making exposition rather than persuasion its typical rhetorical method. However, this judgment has to be modified in terms of the Buddhist answer to question number three.

3) The methodology of rhetoric inevitably develops from its view of human nature. For it is only from our conception of what man is that we can derive a system of motivation. To the Buddhist, it appears that man (taken as an individual) is prone to error, selfish, aggressive, untrustworthy, and governed far more by emotions than by reason. In this respect, Buddhistic rhetoric agrees closely with the rhetoric of Aristotle and his Western followers. This view of the nature of man is implicit in the great care with which Gautama Buddha spelled out the rules for a good life, and the need he felt to urge that they ought to be followed. It is made clearly explicit in the Buddhistic folk-lore, as found in the stories of the *Ramayana* and the *Panchatantra,* which recurrently picture individuals as sly as those found in Aesop's *Fables.* Thus far we may feel that the motive appeals which we in the West use should apply equally well in our dealing with the Buddhists.

Buddhism, however, posits a very different view of human nature than that depicted by the Judeo-Christian tradition. Whereas our culture places great emphasis upon the individuality of every unique soul—leading, for example, to John Locke's doctrine of political competitive freedom—the Buddhistic view, as we have seen, is of an indivisible Over-Soul. To Buddhists, the goal of every individual life is to lose its uniqueness through entrance into Nirvana—the blessed state in which independent existence is no longer a necessity.

4) From these answers to the foregoing questions, we see, then, that different answers to question four emerge in Buddhist rhetoric than those established in the Aristotelian tradition. As speakers we must indeed appeal to the selfishness of man, for such is his earthly nature. But we should not appeal *for* selfishness but *from* it. We should not urge the rewards of individual gain. We should not promise fame, fortune, or any other personal advantages. Insofar as we become Buddhistic rhetoricians, we will recognize selfishness in order to warn against it, rather than to take advantage of it.

Our Western goal is individual achievement; but for the Buddhists, in terms at least of their own deepest traditions, the selfish desire which motivates each of us is not for his own further isolation from reality (by means of enrichment or fame) but, rather, for the merging of our individuality into the infinite richness of indivisible totality.

If this conclusion seems to be contradicted by the competitiveness of much of Buddhist society, as illustrated by the vast wealth of some Indians, we must not forget Gautama Buddha's warning that few are wise enough to seek the "right path." If it seems also to be contradicted by what appears to be the moral and intellectual arrogance of such a man as Krishna Menon, representing India at the United Nations, it is readily apparent that Buddhism offers no great barrier to arrogance. The man who thinks he sees the truth while others persist in error is not notable for humility. Gautama Buddha praises humility, but the ideal or Enlightened man is "He who, for the sake of the living, discriminates and proclaims the truth in regard to all laws."

The chief necessity, then, to enhance the effectiveness of our communication with the Buddhist third of the human race, is to understand that when they talk, or when they listen to us, they interpret any particular aspect of reality in terms of an indivisible whole. The truth they seek is not an explicit account of the fact of a particular instance, but the relationship of that instance to the "continuous aesthetic continuum." Appeals to self-interest they are very likely to interpret as a denial of the basic interest of the self, which is to lose its identity in the universal wholeness. An instance of evil they may seem to dismiss with cavalier indifference, for to them it is but a random and therefore insignificant portion of a desirable whole. Proof that the Communist nations are violating a pledged treaty they may regard as of little consequence, for the context within which the treaty is violated is not the same as that within which it was written. The stability and dependability upon which organized society and all international relations depend they will search for not in short-term agreements but in the long view of the indestructible unity of the universe. Neutralism for them, then, is not a device for bargaining for immediate advantage between two giant contestants but a wholly reasonable and indeed inevitable way of life.

We need not agree with them. We need never surrender our efforts to make them see problems from our own point of view. But we can only talk sensibly with them as we understand how their own minds work.

Chapter 12

CULTURE AND RHETORIC:
AN OVER-VIEW

THE PRECEDING CHAPTERS have dealt with the problem which modern technology (weapons, communication, transportation) has made the most urgent and also the most fundamental of our time. The problem is that the entire human race, for the first time in all history, has been drawn together into one community, sharing one destiny, confronted with the danger of complete destruction—yet has not achieved either a sense of communion or a methodology of creating such a feeling of oneness.

The difficulty, as we have seen, lies in two primary causes of divisiveness. The first is the fact of national sovereignty, which prevents political unity, encourages military antagonisms, and breeds suspicion and hostility. The second lies in deep-seated cultural differences, which result in confusion of understanding even when purposes are similar, and which further lead to unrealized or misunderstood differences rooted in contrary value systems.

In the United States, as in other countries, the past generation has witnessed enormous changes which have altered essentially the nature of group and national relationships. The result is that we are living in an Age of Obsolescence: an age in which the standards and modes of thinking to which we have become solidly attached are hopelessly ineffective for meeting the absolute needs of our newly tightly-intertwined world. All of us who are now middle-aged have grown up in a world of comfortable compartmentalism. We have become habituated to thinking in compartmentalized terms: with nation divided against nation, race against race, wealthy against poor, educated against illiterate, Christian against non-Christian (or against pagan, as we have learned to believe), civilized against savage, weak against strong.

But the compartments have proved worse than useless; they have turned into spawning grounds of hatred, of suspicion, of fear. The problem has thrust itself upon us so massively that it cannot be ignored. But we have not yet learned to understand it, much less to deal with it.

We know the Berlin wall is a dangerous as well as a hideous anachronism. We know that the *Apartheid* policy of the Union of South Africa and our own clumsy resistance to racial integration are diseased remnants of an unrecapturable past. We know that economic aid to under-developed countries is not merely a generous gesture but a growing necessity. We know that neutralism, revolutionism, bloc-voting in the United Nations, and undisciplined violence are inevitable concomitants of the premature but unstoppable creation of multiple independent nations out of many colonialized and generally exploited areas in Africa, Asia, and the Middle East. The fact of yeasty ferment, the reality of the break-down of a once-dependable system of human relationships, and the danger posed for all of us by the unrestrained competitiveness marking this age of rapid change, all of this is far too evident to be ignored. But we do not yet know what to do. The Communists have reacted by building yet another wall—in Berlin. We must somehow bring ourselves to the kind of insight that will permit us to build gateways of friendly communication that will penetrate the many obsolescent walls of psychological, cultural, and political divisiveness, which have also become anachronistic.

The preceding chapters have examined some of the political barriers that make difficult the negotiations among sovereign nations and some of the cultural barriers that obstruct achievement of common understanding. The point of view underlying this discussion is that the problem must be solved *rhetorically*. We must, in other words, deal with it as a problem of persuasion, with our means of persuasion geared to the realities that exist.

A rhetorician is accustomed to analyzing his audience—in this case a world audience. He is accustomed to trying to view all the relevant facts objectively—that is, as they appear to others as well as to himself. He is accustomed, finally, to examining his own purposes—to make sure what he really does want to accomplish, and to determine whether this purpose is both sound and achievable in view of the objective facts and the predisposition of the people to whom his message is being directed.

It is precisely in the realm of rhetoric that we have been most unrealistic in trying to deal with the complex problems of this newly inter-twined globe. Our habits of thought have been too tradition-bound. We have grown up in a culture dominated by the rhetoric of Aristotle and Locke and we have been so successful in our utilization of it that we have been inclined to believe this is not *a* rhetoric but rhetoric itself. We have tended to accept this kind of thinking as though it were the typical mode of thought for the entire human race. Our confidence has been bred by many generations of success—a success that was really based more upon sheer power and wealth than upon its cultural and psychological realism.

Now, for the first time in the long history of Western civilization, we are suddenly (and for many of us ununderstandably) confronted by failure. What we have *known* was the *right* way of dealing with people has incredibly proved to be insufficient. On the whole, we have not yet been willing to concede that it may in fact be *wrong*. We have sought to try harder. We have tried to be generous in interpreting the resistance of the people who refuse to agree with us; but often (in our reaction to the neutralism of India, the enmity of Cuba, and the violent irresponsibility of the Congo, to mention just a few instances) we have become convinced that the nations or peoples we seek to influence are either hopelessly stupid or willfully wicked. They simply refuse to see reason. They violate even their own selfish interests. They refuse cooperation when our sole desire is to help them. They betray us when our generosity in helping them is absolutely unprecedented in international relations. No wonder we are confused.

The suggestion offered in this book is that we need to analyze more thoughtfully the reasons for our failures. When a salesman cannot sell automobiles, he may blame the product, or the price, or the obtuseness of his potential customers. But he becomes a better salesman when he starts to think seriously about his own methods of salesmanship. And he knows that what he must do most surely of all is to devise a new way of presenting his message in terms of the manner of thinking and feeling of his prospects. This is the approach American salesmanship has always used—and the results have been stupendous. But only to a limited extent has this method been used in our approach to the other peoples and nations of the world.

The way the world looks to us is determined in large part by the way in which we have been brought up. The value system of our society becomes the mould within which our minds operate. What seems important to us is precisely that—important *to us*. It may be singularly insignificant to others. If we would communicate across cultural barriers, we must learn what to say and how to say it in terms of the expectations and predispositions of those we want to listen.

Margaret Mead, in "Some Cultural Approaches to Communications Problems" (in Lyman Bryson's *The Communication of Ideas,* 1948), analyzes three different communication systems of three tribes in New Guinea. Although the Arapesh, Manu, and Bali tribes are geographically contiguous, each has a distinctive manner of communication that is correlated with its own economic and social circumstances. All individuals, everywhere, are what Charles Horton Cooley called "reflected looking glass selves"—reflections of their society. As Emile Durkheim wrote in *Rules of Sociological Method* (1898) : "all education is a continuous effort to impose on the child ways of seeing, feeling, and acting which he would not have arrived at spontaneously." The result is that we are far removed from the possibility that "facts are facts, and there's the end of it." Instead, we are concerned with "social facts" —that is, with interpretations of situations and events in terms of social expectations. This largely explains the judgment of Walter Lippmann that "For the most part we do not see first and then define, we define then see." Naturally, people from different cultures see what seem to them to be different facts. This is why it often happens that peoples to whom we talk, or to whom we listen, seem to us to be wildly impractical, or unrealistic, or downright unethical.

Where we have fallen short in our adaptation to them has been in our failure to see that Aristotelianism, Lockianism, and our own religio-ethical beliefs are *ours,* not *theirs.* We have adapted what we do and how we do it—but the very adaptation has consisted largely in a refinement of our own way of thinking and of acting.

We have been slow to listen to the lesson of the cultural anthropologists that the very thought-structure, the basic value-systems, the fundamental manner of perceiving reality all differ—and in significant ways—from people to people, from culture to culture.

The great over-riding fact which we need to accept is that there is no such thing as *a rhetoric* which is common at all; instead there are *many rhetorics*. Peoples in separate cultures and separate nations are concerned about *different* problems; and they have *different* systems of thinking about them. What seems important to us is not necessarily important to everyone. Our logic may not be theirs; and our very faith in rationality may be counter-matched by their faith in irrationality. What we consider proof of a particular proposition, they may consider irrelevant. What we need most of all is a re-education—not just an enlarged, or more systematic, or more thorough education, but an actual substitution of a world-view for the parochial view within which we have been nurtured.

The trend of history is, of course, precisely in this direction. Most of us who may be reading this book grew up on Local Lane, with little interest beyond our own communities. Then the Great Depression and World War II projected us into a change of mental habitat to Main Street, U.S.A., where we began to think naturally and habitually about American rather than local problems. Now the advent of the Space Age, including the development of weapon-systems capable of delivering destruction everywhere, has once again changed our psychological address—this time to Cross-Roads, Earth (shortly to become Cross-Roads, Universe). The new change is already taking place, accelerated by the great increase in world travel, the delivery into our own homes of television news from everywhere, and the constant discussion of world problems in the United Nations and in street-corner conversations.

The change is occurring, but, as always happens, far too slowly and incompletely. Our educational system lags far behind the realities of the changes that are speeding around us. We still are teaching ourselves and our children to view events in traditional ways. We still, in short, are basing our analyses of global questions upon our own Aristotelian rhetorical system, rather than in accordance with a wide range of divergent rhetorics.

SELECTED READINGS

This brief reading list is designed for people who may wish to continue the kind of inquiry indicated by this book. The titles listed represent only a small portion of the many writers to whom I am deeply indebted for information and insights. In general, this list comprises introductory rather than specialized studies.

Armstrong, Hamilton Fish (Editor): *The Foreign Affairs Reader.* New York, Harper, 1947.

Barbara, Dominick A.: *The Art of Listening.* Springfield, Thomas, 1958.

——: *Your Speech Reveals Your Personality.* Springfield, Thomas, 1958.

Benedict, Ruth: *The Chrysanthemum and the Sword.* New York, Houghton, Mifflin, 1946.

Benoit, Hubert: *The Supreme Doctrine: Psychological Studies in Zen Thought.* New York, Viking, 1955.

Berlo, David K.: *The Process of Communications: An Introduction to Theory and Practice.* New York, Holt, Rinehart, and Winston, 1960.

Buck, Pearl: *The Good Earth.* New York, John Day, 1931.

Burtt, E. A. (Editor: *The Teachings of the Compassionate Buddha.* New York, New American Library, Mentor Book, 1955.

Chai, Ch'u, with Chai, Winberg: *Story of Chinese Philosophy.* New York, Washington Square Press, 1961.

Crankshaw, Edward: *Russia and the Russians.* New York, Viking, 1938.

Creel, H. G.: *Chinese Thought from Confucius to Mao Tze-tung.* Chicago, University of Chicago Press, 1953.

——: *Confucius: The Man and the Myth.* New York, John Day, 1949.

Dodds, E. R.: *The Greeks and the Irrational.* Berkeley, University of California Press, 1951.

Durant, Will: *Our Oriental Heritage.* New York, Simon and Schuster, 1935.

Duyvendak, J. J. L.: *The Book of the Way and Its Virtue.* New York, Wisdom of the East Series, 1954.

Estrich, Robert M. and Sperber, Hans: *Three Keys to Language.* New York, Rinehart, 1952.

Fried, Morton H. (Editor): *Readings in Anthropology.* (Two volumes) New York, Crowell, 1959.

Fromm, Erich: *Man for Himself: An Inquiry into the Psychology of Ethics.* New York, Rinehart, 1947.

Goffman, Erving: *The Presentation of the Self in Everyday Life.* New York, Doubleday Anchor Books, 1959.

Hall, Edward T.: *The Silent Language.* New York, Doubleday, 1959.

Hall, Robert A., Jr.: *Linguistics and Your Language.* New York, Doubleday Anchor Books, 1950.

Han, Pyo-Wook: "A Sense of Values: The Basis for Liberty and Democracy in the Far East," *Vital Speeches of the Day, XXIV:*137–139, Dec. 13, 1957.

Hawton, Hector: *Philosophy for Pleasure: An Adventure in Ideas.* New York, Philosophical Library, 1956.

Hayakawa, Samuel I. (Editor): *Language, Meaning, and Maturity.* New York, Harper, 1954.

———: *Our Language and Our World.* New York, Harper, 1959.

Hodgkinson, Harry: *The Language of Communism.* New York, Pitman, 1954.

Hoijer, Harry (Editor): *Language in Culture.* Chicago, University of Chicago Press, 1954.

Holt, Robert T. and van de Velde, Robert W.: *Strategic Psychological Operations and American Foreign Policy.* Chicago, University of Chicago Press, 1960.

Hunter, Edward: *Brain-Washing in Red China: The Calculated Destruction of Men's Minds.* New York, Vanguard, 1951.

Inkeles, Alex: *Public Opinion in Soviet Russia: A Study in Mass Persuasion.* Cambridge, Harvard University Press, 1951.

Joy, C. Turner: *How Communists Negotiate.* New York, Macmillan, 1955.

Kennan, George F.: *American Diplomacy: 1900-1950.* Chicago, University of Chicago Press, 1951.

Klineberg, Otto: "A Science of National Character." *Journal of Social Psychology,* Vol. *XIX:*147–162, 1944.

Köhler, Wolfgang: *Gestalt Psychology.* New York, Liveright, 1947.

Lasswell, Harold D.: *World Politics and Personal Insecurity: A Contribution to Political Psychiatry,* New York, McGraw-Hill, 1935.

Latourette, Kenneth Scott: *A Short History of the Far East.* New York, Macmillan, 1946.

Lee, Irving J.: *Customs and Crises in Communication.* New York, Harper, 1954.

Legge, J.: *Texts of Taoism.* (Two volumes) Oxford, University Press, n. d.

Lewin, Kurt: *Field Theory in Social Science.* New York, Harper, 1951.

Linton, Ralph: *Cultural Background of Personality*. New York, Appleton-Century, 1945.

Lippmann, Walter: *Essays in the Public Philosophy*. Boston, Little, Brown, 1955.

——: *Public Opinion*. New York, Macmillan, 1922.

Mead, Margaret: "Some Cultural Approaches to Communications Problems," and "A Case History in Cross-National Communications," in *The Communication of Ideas*, Lyman Bryson, Editor, New York, Harper, pp. 9–26 and 209–230, 1948.

Nehru, Jawaharlal: *The Discovery of India*. London, Meridian Books, 1946.

Newman, John B.: "A Rationale for a Definition of Communication," *Journal of Communication*, Vol. X:115–124, Sept., 1960.

Nicolson, Harold George: *Diplomacy*. London, Butterworth, 1939.

——: *The Evolution of Diplomatic Method*. London, Constable, 1954.

——: *The Congress of Vienna: A Study in Allied Unity, 1812-1822*. New York, Harcourt, Brace, 1946.

Northrop, F. S. C.: *The Meeting of East and West*. New York, Macmillan, 1946.

Ogden, G. K., and Richards, I. A.: *The Meaning of Meaning*. New York, Harcourt, Brace, 1923.

Oliver, Robert T.: "American Foreign Policy in the Midst of World Revolution: The Permanent and the Transient in an Age of Obsolescence." *Vital Speeches of the Day, Vol.* XXVIII:101–104, Dec. 1, 1961.

——: "Northeast Asia: Vital Flank in the Cold War." *Discourse,* Vol. *II*:95–104, April, 1959.

——: "Speech as Influence," in *Psychological and Psychiatric Aspects of Speech and Hearing*. Dominick A. Barbara, Editor. Springfield, Thomas, pp. 27–41, 1960.

——: *Syngman Rhee: The Man Behind the Myth*. New York, Dodd, Mead, rev., 1960.

——: "Ten Factors in the Global Struggle." *Vital Speeches of the Day,* Vol. *XXII*:207–209, Jan. 15, 1956.

Parker, Charles H.: *Dog Eats Moon*. Pittsfield, Mass., Greylock, 1950.

Polanyi, Michael: *Personal Knowledge: Towards a Post-Critical Philosophy*. Chicago, University of Chicago Press, 1958.

Riesman, David, Glazer, Nathan, and Denney, Reuel: *The Lonely Crowd*. New Haven, Yale University Press, 1950.

Rosinger, Lawrence K. (Editor) : *The State of Asia: A Contemporary Survey*. New York, Knopf, 1951.

Sands, William Franklin: *Undiplomatic Memories: The Far East, 1896-1904*. London, John Hamilton, n.d.

Sinclair, Angus: *The Conditions of Knowing: An Essay Towards a Theory of Knowledge*. New York, Harcourt, Brace, 1951.

Vaihinger, Hans: *The Philosophy of 'As If': A System of the Theoretical, Practical, and Religious Fictions of Mankind*. Translated by C. K. Ogden. London, Routledge and Kegan Paul, 1924.

Waley, Arthur: *The Way and Its Power: A Study of the Tao Te Ching and Its Place in Chinese Thought*. New York, Grove Press, n. d.

Ware, James R. (Translator): *The Sayings of Mencius*. New York, New American Library, Mentor Book, 1960.

Watson, Jeanne, and Lippit, Ronald: "Cross-Cultural Experience as a Source of Attitude Change." *Journal of Conflict Resolutions, II:* 1958.

Watts, Alan W.: *The Legacy of Asia and Western Man*. London, John Murray, 1937.

——: *The Way of Zen*. New York, Pantheon Press, 1957.

Whorf, Benjamin Lee: *Language, Thought, and Reality*. Edited by John B. Carroll. New York, Wiley, 1956.

Wilson, Hugh R.: *The Education of a Diplomat*. New York, Longmans, Green, 1938.

Winance, Eleutherius: *The Communist Persuasion: A Personal Experience of Brainwashing*. New York, P. J. Kenedy & Sons, 1959.

Yutang, Lin, Editor: *The Wisdom of China and India*. New York, Random House, 1942.

INDEX